Public Library Administrators'
Planning Guide to Automation

OCLC Library, Information, and Computer Science Series

Public Library Administrators' Planning Guide to Automation

Donald J. Sager

6565 Frantz Road
Dublin, Ohio 43017-0702

ISBN: 0-933418-35-3 (Series)
     0-933418-43-4

1   2   3   4   5   6   I   86   85   84   83

Contents

Foreword

Drawing upon both his research while serving as an OCLC
Distinguished Visiting Scholar and his extensive
administrative experience, which includes the directorships
at the Chicago Public Library, the Public Library of
Columbus and Franklin County, the Mobile Public Library,
the Kingston (NY) Area Library, and the Elyria (OH) Public
Library, Donald J. Sager has succeeded in achieving his
goal to provide public library administrators with a
planning guide to automation that is both comprehensive and
practical.

Thoughtful readers of this guide will be able to readily
associate pertinent planning principles with the automation
decision-making process. Indeed, the <u>Public Library
Administrators' Planning Guide to Automation</u> is a manual
which leads the concerned administrator step-by-step
through the maze of factors that must be identified and
evaluated when considering the potential benefits of
library automation.

The guide begins with a thorough discussion of
problem-centered responsibilities. It includes a useful
prioritization table as an aid to assigning priorities to
automation strategies. Sager emphasizes that the
identification of goals and the decision to automate can
best be achieved by a planning committee. This is a
suggestion with which most experienced public library
administrators agree.

Quite properly, the author acknowledges the influence of automation in shaping the future of public libraries of all sizes. Automation provides both foundation and gateway in creating an environment for exploiting the potential benefits of modern computer and telecommunications technology and services.

The emphasis placed on the costs and benefits of automation is practical and appropriate. Any administrator who has grappled with the preparation of requests for proposals (RFPs) will especially appreciate the value of this planning guide as a reference source and checklist for use in RFP formulation. The quality and detail of responses to an RFP cannot be overstated in the automation decision-making process.

When estimating automation, software, hardware, maintenance, and communications costs, other cost factors related to automation often fail to receive adequate initial attention. In this connection, chapter 7, "Estimating Automation Costs," should be required reading for any public library administrator contemplating automation. It is particularly comprehensive, addressing such topics as decision-making expenses, facilities, furniture, conversion expenses, and replacement costs.

The second volume in OCLC's Library, Information, and Computer Science Series, Donald J. Sager's planning guide to automation is a primer for public library administrators committed to effective use of available resources.

Keith Doms, Director

The Free Library of Philadelphia

Acknowledgments

Special appreciation in the preparation of this guide is
due Rowland Brown, president and CEO of OCLC Online
Computer Library Center, Inc., who invited the author to
study the needs of public libraries relative to automation
and provided the opportunity to do so by appointing the
author Visiting Scholar at OCLC in 1982. Appreciation is
also due Dr. Neal Kaske, director of OCLC's Office of
Research, who provided much guidance and encouragement
during the period when this guide was formulated. The
author is indebted to the OCLC Library staff for their
efforts in procuring so many resources and to the staff of
the OCLC Office of Research, who provided many suggestions
which have improved this guide.

The author is also grateful to those library administrators
who provided their advice on methods which would improve
the application of automation to public libraries during a
series of focused-group interviews held during the
midwinter conference of the American Library Association in
Denver in January 1982. The common thread which ran
through those discussions was the need for a simple guide
which would help administrators to plan more effectively
for automation and permit them to estimate more accurately
the costs involved with conversion, implementation, and
maintenance. It is hoped that this guide will provide some
assistance to administrators in that regard.

Introduction

Discussions with selected public library administrators from cities, suburbs, and rural areas have revealed the need for a simple guide that would aid in estimating costs for automated services and establish basic techniques for planning for automation in the context of the public library. While a great deal has been published on the subject of automation, specifically automation in libraries, it is often technical in nature and does not focus on the elements of greatest concern to administrators in small- and medium-sized public libraries.

The most recent survey of public libraries by the National Center for Educational Statistics reveals that more than 90 percent of all public libraries serve populations of less than 50,000 and operate with budgets of less than $400,000. [1]   In fact, 64 percent of all public libraries serve populations of 10,000 or less and have operating budgets of $50,000 or less. Most of these institutions lack the resources to effectively analyze and assess the benefits and costs of newer technology.

The purpose of this guide is to establish some simple procedures that will aid public library administrators, particularly in small- and medium-sized institutions, to study the potential benefits of automation, examine the alternatives for implemention, estimate the costs for any conversion necessary and for operation, and compare these expenses with the library's present procedures. The reader will not find the answers to questions on automation for a specific library. Rather, the reader will find methods that will permit those answers to be obtained.

This guide was greatly influenced by <u>A Planning Process for Public Libraries</u>,[2] which sets forth a number of steps that will help American public libraries to gather information essential to formulate a sound general plan of public services for a community of any size. That manual is recommended as background for any library administrator, and it is hoped that this guide will serve as a brief supplement to it. Accordingly, there will be references to this larger manual at several points in this guide.

The second chapter of this guide discusses priorities in planning for automation; it was developed based on focused-group interviews with a sampling of library directors from various size institutions. These discussions revealed some concern over how a library should begin to automate. Most librarians believe the first step is to develop a machine-readable database of the institution's bibliographic records. Many public library administrators feel their library's greatest need is for online circulation control, and they may bypass this first step with the intention of using only brief bibliographic records in their online circulation system.

Other library administrators believe that automation can only be justified as a means of solving specific problems in the operation of the institution. Some administrators also believe that, rather than starting to totally automate the library in a logical, phased plan, limited library revenues may better be applied to save staff time by converting only the most labor-intensive activities. The second chapter of this guide discusses the alternatives and establishes a framework for decision making.

Judging by the number of conference programs on automation, the application of this technology to libraries is of considerable interest to librarians. Computerization is viewed positively in the profession. Unfortunately, many libraries often proceed without a sound set of goals and objectives. To clarify this need, the third chapter focuses on setting goals for automation. This chapter does not suggest the goals that should be adopted for a specific public library, but it does review methods that can be employed by an administrator to set specific goals which would be appropriate. These methods include involving those who have a stake in this change.

Despite the relative decline in the cost of computerization, many libraries will find that it is beyond their
capability to finance the purchase of equipment and the
cost of conversion to a new system and still afford to
maintain and operate the new equipment. In fact, there is
some evidence that unilateral adoption of automation by an
institution may be undesirable for several reasons other
than cost. Chapter 4 is designed to aid library
administrators in evaluating the potential advantages and
disadvantages of cooperating with other libraries in
automating services and procedures.

Discussions with library administrators reveal that cost
still presents the greatest single barrier to computerization. The fifth chapter attempts to define the various
financing methods that are commonly available to public
institutions and allows the user to estimate the relative
expenses associated with these methods. Probably the most
common methods employed by libraries are outright purchase
or lease. There are, however, other methods which are
often used by business and industry, and these may be
adaptable by libraries.

A review of the literature on public libraries published
during the past ten years reveals that very little exists
on cost analysis for even the most common procedures and
services in these institutions. A special task force has
been established by the Public Library Association to
develop some specific procedures that can be applied by
library administrators to standardize the measurement of
these costs, and in the future these procedures will be
available for use. There is an immediate need, nonetheless, for some guidelines which will help administrators
compare their costs for present operations with estimated
costs for automation. Accordingly, chapter 6 addresses
this subject, based on the limited amount of literature
that has been published on cost analysis during the past
several years. This chapter should be considered an
interim guide pending the work of the PLA Special Task
Force on Cost Analysis.

The seventh chapter provides guidelines for estimating
costs for automation. It contains sections on the more
common types of automation in use among public libraries.
Each section itemizes factors that should be included in

arriving at total expenses for hardware and software,
conversion to the application, maintenance, and other
costs. Costs are, however, only one element to be
considered in automation.

For many years the watchword in industry and government has
been accountability. While that remains of critical
concern to the American public, there is also increasing
emphasis on value and reliability. Improved quality of
service, improved accessibility, and a host of other
benefits are hard to measure in terms of their impact on
the operation of any institution. For that reason, they
are often put aside; that is unfortunate, since these
factors are often among the major advantages of automation
in public libraries. They merit attention by any
administrator who is considering the application of newer
technology to any size institution. For this reason, the
final chapter contains some additional information on the
most common factors that should be considered by library
administrators in planning for automation and suggests some
methods that can be used by administrators to weigh
elements other than cost in reaching decisions.

2

Establishing Priorities in Automation

One of the more common problems faced in automation is
deciding where to begin. It is possible to automate only a
single process or to develop a plan which will lead to
total automation of the procedures and services of the
library. Many administrators fear that automating only a
single process will make it difficult to integrate that
procedure into other automated processes in subsequent
years. Worse, it may become necessary to rebuild a
database or go through some expensive technical conversion
to allow more effective use of an automated process.

Design of a plan for total automation, on the other hand,
may delay the application of new technology to solve an
immediate problem. For example, a staff shortage at the
circulation desk and increased circulation may dictate the
need for the purchase of an online circulation control
system. While it might be desirable to take a number of
preliminary steps before installation of an online
circulation system, such as building a full bibliographic
database of the institution's holdings in machine-readable
form, that may be a luxury the institution can ill afford
when other priorities exist. Moreover, taking time to
establish an elaborate plan for automating the library when
only a single application is being considered may seem
redundant, and it could result in the conclusion that
automation is too costly.

It has been the experience of many libraries, however, that
piecemeal automation results in greater expense, public
frustration, and poor use of staff time. Automation should

be based on a logical plan, even if only one application is
currently being considered. A plan for automation will
provide assurance to governing bodies, staff, and the
public that careful thought has been given to how individual applications of automation can be integrated with other
steps in the future. A plan for automation will permit
priorities to be established on a sound basis. It will
provide the answer for those library administrators who
need to determine where they should begin.

2.1 Problem-centered Priorities

The library administrator or the planning committee must
start by listing those problems which it hopes can be
solved through automation. The process of setting goals,
described in the next chapter, should produce such a list.
No effort need be made at this stage to rank these
problems, which as stated, may represent the general goals
of the institution. To these problems should be added any
goals which do not relate solely to the resolution of
existing problems or service deficiencies. These may
consist of future needs of the community as perceived by
the planning committee, and they would probably tend to be
considered of low priority, since planning tends to focus
primarily on goals which would satisfy the most immediate
needs.

Once this list has been established, the administrator or
committee must identify the real nature of the problem.
This is essential to ensure the institution does not
transfer the source of many of its existing problems into
the automated application. For example, the typical public
library usually has collected a substantial file of
delinquent borrowers over the years. Many of these patrons
may have moved or passed away, or the library may have
simply made errors in its manual system. To transfer this
information from a manual file into an automated file will
not solve the library's delinquency problem. In fact, the
problem may be compounded, because a patron may be more
effectively stopped with an automated circulation system.
If the delinquency record is in error, public relations
problems may develop. In some instances, such problems can
be resolved by a policy recommendation from the library
board or a change in operating procedures. For example, a

delinquency file laced with errors or out-of-date
information may simply be purged, or an arbitrary limit
(such as only transferring records established in the last
two years and discarding earlier records) set as a
guideline for transferring delinquent information from the
manual file to the machine-readable database.

It is commonly assumed by library administrators that
automation will improve the quality of the institution's
bibliographic records. However, if the institution has
poor-quality cataloging, it will be of little value to
transfer this to a computerized database. Some steps must
be taken to correct cataloging deficiencies before or
during conversion to a computerized catalog, since records
are only as good as the quality of information used to
generate them.

There is also a question regarding how much of the
collection still exists or should be retained in the
future. Any public library that transfers its
bibliographic records into a union catalog in an automated
form, or to an online circulation system, without
inventorying and weeding its collection in advance, will be
transferring some of its current problems into the new
technology. It will be perpetuating these problems, not
solving them. Patrons will continue to seek books no
longer in the collection, and records will be maintained on
books which no longer satisfy the needs of the community.
These unnecessary records represent expensive overhead for
the library, in terms of both patron and staff time. In
addition there are real costs for converting and then
maintaining these records in machine-readable form.

There is a simple word for these miscellaneous problems--
garbage. Besides preparing a list of goals and problems,
the administrator or committee must also prepare a list of
steps to be taken to eliminate this garbage. In some
instances, there may be overlap and duplication between
items on these lists. These items logically become
priorities in the library's automation plan. Some of these
steps can be converted to objectives which can be matched
against the associated list of automation strategies. In
some instances, these steps preparatory to automation can

be resolved by a policy recommendation from the library board or changes in operating procedures.

Elimination of deficiencies may lead an administrator or planning committee to conclude that automation is not needed. Once the preparatory steps are completed, such as cleaning up the card catalog, performing an inventory, and eliminating outdated circulation records, the present procedures can be continued because the library's goals or problems have been satisfied. If this is true, then the planning process was effective and helpful. Automation is not the solution to every problem the library experiences, and the steps which have to be taken in preparation for automation represent good library management.

The administrator must balance what automation can accomplish compared with the future maintenance of these manual files. If the collection or other records can be effectively maintained manually and not deteriorate to the state they were in before the upgrading effort, then automation may not be needed. On the other hand, if growth in the collection or in usage is anticipated, or if it is anticipated that staff and revenues will not be sufficient to cope with existing or projected levels of use, then it would be well to consider automating that process to ensure that the effort is not wasted and to maintain the quality of records and services.

The product of the administrator's or planning committee's effort should now consist of one list of problems and goals and a second list of preparatory steps. These two lists should be merged, with the preparatory steps appropriate to each goal or problem grouped under those headings and restated as objectives. In many instances, these preparatory steps will appear under several goals, and it will be possible for the committee or administrator to measure the relative importance of that activity and its contribution to the library's overall automation plan.

2.2 Factors in Establishing Priorities

Once the lists have been merged, it is possible to establish priorities objectively. Whether this is done by the administrator or by a planning committee, a simple

process involving weighted factors may be useful. Certain
strategies may clearly stand out as the planning process in
automation proceeds, making this weighting process seem
unnecessary. However, the administrator or committee could
have personal biases that interfere in the process of
setting priorities objectively. Since implementing the
plan will almost certainly involve the use of public money
and, therefore, be subject to public review, it is
desirable to employ a logical process to establish
priorities to reduce the likelihood of criticism that
strategies and priorities were established arbitrarily.

Ranking automation strategies can be achieved by
identifying a limited number of goals important to improved
library service in the community and assigning weights to
each as a measure of its relative importance. These goals
may be extracted from the institution's long-range plan and
may be the broad goals which the board and the
administration have adopted, such as improved public
service, lower costs of operation, etc. If the institution
has a complex long-range plan with many detailed goals, it
might be best to identify the more critical ones,
preferably five or six, or attempt to subsume several
specific ones under a broad general heading, such as more
effective use of personnel resources. If the institution
lacks a long-range plan, then the administrator or planning
committee should list those abstract or practical points
which have most frequently served as the basis for
decisions by the library board, administration, or staff.

Once such a list is prepared, the next step should be to
create a table which lists all of these goals across the
top, with separate columns for each. Assign a weight to
each. It can be 1 to 5 (1 = low, 5 = high), 1 to 10, or
whatever seems appropriate. These goals do not have to be
ranked. It is possible that all will have equal weights
assigned to them, as do the goals listed across the top of
table 1, or one or two may be given greater weights than
the others.

Next, consider each library service; list all of the
services being considered for automation in abbreviated
fashion down the left side of the table, and assign either
a value of 1, 2, or 3 to each column headed by a weighted
goal. A weight of 1 should be entered in the column if

automation will make little or no contribution to that
goal. A weight of 2 should be entered if automation will
make a contribution; a 3 should be entered if automation
will make a significant contribution to that goal. This
process should be repeated in turn for each of the goals in
the library's plan.

TABLE 1. Prioritization Table

| | GOALS | | | |
	Quality Service (5)	Efficient Operations (5)	Accessibility (5)	Accuracy (5)	Weighted Total
AUTOMATION OF SERVICE					
Online Circulation Control	3	3	3	3	60
Online Reference	2	2	1	1	30
Acquisitions	1	3	1	2	35
Serials	1	3	3	2	45
Word Processing	1	2	1	2	30
Public Online Catalog	3	2	3	2	50

The example shown as table 1 assumes that establishing
online circulation was identified as a strategy, and the
goals selected by the administrator or committee were
quality service, efficient operations, accessibility, and

accuracy.   All were considered to have an equal weight of
5.   The committee concluded that the circulation system
would make a significant contribution in all categories and
assigned a 3 to each column.   Multiplying the weight of
each goal (5) by the value assigned to the strategy
contribution to that goal (3), and adding the products of
these operations determines the weighted total.   In this
example, the sum for circulation control is 60.

The same process can be employed for all of the goals, and
it should be possible for a ranking or prioritization to be
established for the strategies.

2.3 Revision of Priorities

If any changes in priorities have occurred, the
administrator or committee should alter the schedules
contained in the first draft of the automation plan.   In
small- and medium-sized public libraries, the same
department or staff may be required to perform several
functions to prepare for automation, while maintaining
their normal public service responsibilities.   The
priorities thus establish a natural sequence of work which
will lead to completion of the automation plan.

It is particularly important that the persons or
departments responsible for these tasks be involved in
planning and establishing priorities.   If, for various
reasons, that is not possible, then it is essential they be
aware of the tasks and deadlines and agree with them.   No
plan can be successfully adopted without effective
participation and good communication.   This is particularly
true in terms of meeting schedules.

2.4 Summary

Even if the library is planning to automate only one
function or service, it is desirable to establish an
overall plan for automation to ensure the automated
function is designed to integrate with other services which
may be automated in the future.   The design of a basic plan
for automation will answer the question of where the
library should start and will avoid piecemeal applications

which require rebuilding of databases or expensive
technical conversions.

Priorities can be more logically established through an
overall plan. The first step in establishing priorities is
to list all the problems the library is experiencing that
might be corrected through the application of automation
and to add to this list those goals in service which relate
to future needs in the community. Following this, the
various steps which must be taken by the institution to
prepare for automating each function or service must be
identified. Succeeding chapters in this guide should
assist the administrator or the planning committee in
implementing this process.

The two lists should be merged, with the steps required for
conversion to a particular application grouped under that
application, and then restated as objectives. Next, a set
of weighted factors which contribute to improved public
library service should be created. These factors might be
extracted from the library's general, long-range
development plan, or they might be based on the
philosophies of the library in providing sound service to
the community.

A decision table should be established as an aid to
assigning priorities to automation strategies, with the
abbreviated strategies (expressed as automation of a
specific activity) located on the left side of the table in
separate rows. Goals weighted on a scale of 1-5 or 1-10
should be aligned across the top of the table in separate
columns; a score of 1-3 can then be used to determine which
strategies contribute the most to the advancement of those
goals. This approach to establishing priorities may not be
required because of natural priorities perceived by the
administrator or the planning committee, but it does assist
in making objective determinations and can be used to
justify decisions.

Finally, once priorities have been established for these
automation strategies, the preliminary schedules in the
plan should be altered to reflect these priorities.
Personnel who will be required to approve and implement the
priorities should be involved in determining them.
Communication is essential for effective implementation.

3

Identifying Goals in Automation

Whether or not an institution elects to automate, the decision should be reached by those who will be most affected by the outcome; that is, it should be reached in a participatory fashion. An administrator often assumes full responsibility for that decision because such decision making is believed to be appropriate to the role of the administrator of an organization. The administrator is assumed to have the training, experience, and more importantly, the time to research the alternatives, costs, and benefits. While that is generally true, it is equally true that the administrator has the responsibility to marshal all of the resources which are available to aid in reaching conclusions which will affect the services and procedures of the institution.

Since the administrator's responsibility includes marshaling appropriate resources, the first step in automation planning should be to establish a committee that will involve those who will be affected by the automation. The committee can then weigh the various advantages and disadvantages of automation and identify goals and objectives appropriate for the library. The third step is to integrate these goals with the general development plan for the library.

3.1 The Automation Planning Committee

It is often assumed that any committee should know its purpose from its title. At least that appears to be the

case, based on the large numbers of committees that exist
in libraries today and the absence of clear charges of
responsibility to those committees. If a library
administrator or board is considering automation and elects
to establish a planning committee for that purpose, then
the responsibilities of the committee should be stated with
a simple, clearly written charge.

Several elements should be included. First, a measurable,
specific goal should be stated. A committee may be charged
with completion of a report on whether the library should
automate its circulation procedures. Such a report is
specific and can be measured. If no report is generated by
the committee, the goal has not been met.

Second, a specific time frame should be included in the
charge. If this is not done, there will be confusion or
uncertainty as to when the product should be completed.

Third, the charge should state the audience and to whom the
product should be delivered. For example, if the committee
is to prepare recommendations for the board or library
administrator or some other public official, this should be
clearly stated.

Once the charge has been prepared for a committee, the next
step should be to define the composition of the committee.
As previously stated, it should consist of those who will
be directly affected by the decision. That could include
representatives of the staff, the board, city or county
administration and, on occasion, even the public, depending
upon the application being considered and its relative
impact on expenditures and services. There is no formula
which can be applied other than to ensure that
participation is obtained from those who will have to
approve, implement, and use the application. The size of
the committee may also vary, depending upon the scope of
the decision. Automating payroll may include only a few
people, while the design of a total automation program
would require a more extensive committee membership.

Experience has shown that as committees exceed more than 12
people they become less effective and committee members
find it difficult to contribute to discussion and
consideration of the topic. If an institution is

considering a very complex issue in automation that may
require input from a substantial number of sources, it
might be well to establish a series of subcommittees whose
chairs are members of an overall steering committee.

To be effective, the committee should have adequate support
from the library administration. A Planning Process for
Public Libraries recommends providing such support through
creation of a position titled Data Coordinator. This
person provides needed resources, handles committee meeting
minutes, and organizes information so that it can be
quickly digested by the members of the committee. Whether
or not a data coordinator is created for the automation
planning committee, someone from the library staff should
be charged with the responsibility of assisting the
committee and relieving it of those tasks which delay or
hinder its work.

Some libraries have found it desirable to employ the
services of a facilitator or consultant during the planning
process. This may be an effective way to use a
professional automation consultant. Rather than hiring an
outside consultant to study the library's needs and submit
a report, it may be more useful to have the consultant
serve as a technical advisor, provide cost estimates, and
brief the planning committee on the alternatives to
implement automation. The members of the committee can
thus be given greater insight, feel more involved, and
avoid prescriptive solutions which may be inappropriate for
their institution.

Whether or not the committee employs an outside facilitator
or consultant, the most important member of the committee
is its chairperson. The chairperson may or may not be the
chief administrator, but is that person who has the
greatest responsibility to ensure input, participation, and
effective progress in the completion of the committee's
charge. The chairperson should be carefully chosen by the
board and/or the administrator and should have those skills
essential for effective use of the group process. While a
technical background would be helpful, it is not as
critical as leadership skills and communications ability.

3.2 Problem-centered Planning

The origins of many institutional goals are often the
problems its staff experience in providing the ongoing
services of the institution. There is nothing wrong with
this and, in fact, most libraries would benefit by
periodically examining their long-term goals to ensure some
steps are being taken to correct recurring problems. But
goals should also be designed to guide the library toward
developing services needed in the future and to anticipate
and avoid problems which are likely to arise. The
difficulty is predicting what community needs will exist in
the future and how automation can be employed in satisfying
those needs.

A Planning Process for Public Libraries suggests collecting
both primary and secondary data to use as a basis for
planning. Primary data include surveys of present and
desired needs; secondary data involve the use and analysis
of census information and other locally developed business
and population surveys. Those techniques are equally
applicable in planning for automation, but they should not
be initiated until some preliminary goals are established.
The committee should begin by defining some initial
problems which could be corrected through automation,
identifying what is required in terms of data (including
the cost of alternative solutions to the problem), then
enlarging the goals for automation as information is
analyzed and other potential applications are discovered.

The reason for this approach is that unless the library is
fortunate enough to have either a consultant or staff
familiar with the potential of automation to improve
services, it will design a very limited set of goals. It
might be best to recognize this reality at the start and
let the planning objectives expand as the committee
increases its knowledge of the subject.

3.3 Goals

Goals are usually defined as measurable achievements that
can be attained through the completion of one or more
preliminary objectives. They tend to be broad in nature.
Automation of a function, such as circulation control, is

more properly termed a strategy. Although it will require
a series of steps or objectives before it is achieved, it
is a means to an end--better circulation control--not the
end itself.

Some planners believe that goals should be designed so they
can never be fully achieved. The goals then function as an
incentive to the organization. Others suggest certain
goals should be ongoing, such as the improvement of
services, and always in transition. The problem with these
philosophies is that it becomes difficult to measure
whether the institution is making any progress if goals are
unattainable or ongoing. If the institution cannot measure
its progess toward achieving its goals and plans, then
those goals and plans are of limited value.

One approach to goal definition is to examine those
problems the library faces and to restate those problems as
goals. Thus, the establishment of an automated reserve
system might serve as a strategy, based on problems which
the institution faces in promptly satisfying patron
reserves, with the goal being improved reserve services.
Another example might be the implementation of online
cataloging to meet the goal of eliminating a large
cataloging backlog.

3.4 Objectives

The specific steps which a library takes toward achieving
its goals are properly defined as objectives. In the
hierarchy that represents a long-range plan, these
objectives form the vital link between consideration of
alternatives appropriate to a goal and achievement of that
goal. There are several important elements in formulating
effective objectives.

First, an objective should represent only one task. If
several tasks must be completed to achieve a goal, they
should be written as several objectives.

Second, like the original charge to the committee, the
objective should contain a schedule and target date for
completion of the task. If the objective is open ended,
there is a lack of precision which will render the plan

ineffective. A committee which lacks familiarity with
automation may find it difficult to establish a schedule
for certain steps. If this is so, the information should
be collected from vendors, from other libraries, and from
the literature, and the schedule added once that
information is available. The committee may create a
preliminary schedule and then modify it once data are
received.

A third element essential to the development of sound
objectives is the designation of a person, firm, or
department to carry out the objectives. The failure of
many plans is often due to a lack of certainty as to who is
responsible for carrying out specific activities.
Assigning a person or department responsibility for
completion of the objective will also allow the committee
to identify where critical elements of the workload are
assigned and ensure better distribution of the work.

3.5 Strategies

There is rarely only one way to satisfy an objective; this
is particularly true in complex operations involving
automation. For example, there are scores of ways for a
library to create a COM (computer output microform) catalog
or convert to an online circulation system. A strategy is
an alternative that an institution may take to satisfy
first an objective and, subsequently, a goal.

Strategies are particularly valuable in identifying the
more economical and rapid methods which will result in the
completion of a variety of tasks. There are several
critical elements which are part of good strategies.
First, the library must be able to collect all the facts
necessary to assess the value of a proposed strategy. If
it cannot, then the strategy has limited value and may best
be eliminated from consideration.

It is in developing its list of strategies that the
committee most frequently will need additional information
or data. For example, evaluation of the use of a shelf
list as a source of current bibliographic information for a
COM catalog must be based on the existence of a complete,
current shelf list within the library. The evaluation,

therefore, requires an appraisal of this file as a basis for this particular strategy.

A second basic element in planning strategies is determining the person or department that will have responsibility for implementation. Just as the written objective must include the name of the person or department that will be responsible for its implementation, a strategy must also include this information. Some strategies can be eliminated at the outset if sufficient staff will not exist to convert and maintain a specified process.

Finally, a strategy should also contain a schedule and/or completion date. This ensures the viability of a strategy. It is pointless, for example, to propose that one person perform all of the steps necessary to automate a process during the same period that other duties require the full attention of the same person.

Strategies require the committee to approach goals and objectives based on realities and future probabilities. Planning strategies transform the process into a practical evaluation of existing resources and allow the employment of those resources. It also forces the elimination or modification of goals and objectives when the resources do not exist or cannot be supplied.

An array of strategies should always be maintained even after a specific strategy has been identified as the most desirable one to satisfy an objective. As that strategy is used, it may prove ineffective, or conditions may change and another strategy can be selected from those identified. A strategy list may also be useful to other libraries. They may adopt from the list a strategy to satisfy their individual needs, even though the strategy is not applicable at the library compiling such a list.

3.6 Integration of Library Service and Automation Goals

If the library does not have a set of goals and objectives for improving its services, then it should invest the time necessary to create such a plan. Automation cannot be effectively employed in a vacuum. Automation is not an end in itself; it is only one means a library can use to

improve its services and satisfy present and future
community needs. A study of trends and the use of patron
surveys will frequently be helpful in identifying these
future needs. Again, A Planning Process for Public
Libraries is suggested as a useful guide.

Assuming that general goals exist for the library, it is
essential for the automation planning committee to
familiarize itself with those goals. If a committee for
the development of a long-range plan for the library
exists, then the automation planning committee might
logically and effectively function as a subcommittee to
ensure that its plans dovetail with the overall plan for
the institution. Those segments of the plan which are
related to automation should be integrated into the
automation planning committee's goals. Some of the
objectives and strategies for implementing the general
long-range plan may also suggest other areas where
automation may be effectively employed.

New initiatives for service should be considered in the
context of the library's general long-range plan. If
emphasis is upon youth services, public service personal
computers or computer-assisted instruction might be
employed in an effort to attract that clientele. Where the
thrust is upon expanding the branch library program, the
strategy should consider whether the capacity of the
automated systems can be adjusted. Where emphasis is upon
closer cooperation with local libraries in the sharing of
resources, consideration might be given to construction of
a shared database of bibliographic records in machine-
readable form, either an online or COM catalog.

3.7 The Future of Automation

It is rare to see an application in the library field which
results in the design of a new piece of computer hardware.
Generally, library applications evolve as the profession
grasps the significance of new technology and adapts it for
use in a library setting. The market is too small to
command investment in research and development of new
hardware exclusive to libraries, and there is no evidence
that this situation will change in the future.

It is usually the software that can be made library
specific. Planning should consider that there will
probably be no limitations of a technical nature, but there
may well be economic constraints which limit the use of
computers by libraries. A single library may never be able
to afford to commission the development of software
specific to a particular application. However, a
manufacturer or firm may take the risk and invest heavily
in research and development for a software product with the
intention of recovering the costs by marketing it to other
libraries with similar needs. As costs for development
increase, there will be fewer firms willing to take that
risk. A more practical alternative would be the pooling of
resources by a group of libraries. Chapter 4 of this guide
reviews the relative advantages and disadvantages of such
cooperative applications of automation.

As computers continue to grow in influence, it is safe to
assume that the public will become more conversant with
computers and better prepared to access the library's
services through direct use of a system, rather than
through an intermediary. Accordingly, long-range planning
for the application of computers should consider the
probability of greater public access, increased traffic,
increased terminal capabilities, and the ability of
computers to handle ever greater numbers of terminals.

3.8 Summary

The identification of goals for the library and the
decision to automate can best be achieved in a
participatory fashion. Establishing a committee consisting
of 12 or fewer persons representing staff, the board, local
government and, on occasion, the community would be the
best approach for developing an overall plan, but the size
and composition will depend upon the project under
consideration. The critical element in the selection of
committee members should be the inclusion of those who will
have to approve and implement the project and use it. The
committee should have a clear charge which will note the
product expected, when it is due, and who should receive
it.

A plan for automation should consist of goals, which are
defined as broadly stated achievements that can be measured
to determine progress. The plan should also consist of
objectives and strategies. Objectives are clearly stated
tasks, completion of which will lead to the satisfaction of
related goals. Strategies are alternative methods to
complete related objectives. Both objectives and
strategies should contain a schedule and identify which
individual or department should complete the task.

Goals are often restated solutions to problems or
deficiencies in service which the library staff have
identified. However, an effort should be made to ensure
that the automation plan includes goals which will satisfy
the future needs of the library and the community.

Effort should be made to integrate automation goals into
the general long-range plans of the library. It is
recommended that the institution develop a general
long-range plan (if one has not already been established)
based on A Planning Process for Public Libraries.
Projecting the future of automation is difficult, given the
dynamic nature of the computer science field, but plans
should be based on expanding technical capabilities,
cooperative design of software applications, and greater
public use of computers.

4

Cooperation Among Libraries

Many libraries assume they will never be able to
computerize and ignore the opportunity available through
cooperation with other public or academic, special, or
school libraries. Indeed, the National Center for
Educational Statistics determined in its 1977-1978 survey
that 64 percent of all public libraries possess annual
budgets of $50,000 or less, and the administrators of those
institutions may feel hard-pressed to proceed with
automation using only their individual financial resources.
Yet the literature is filled with examples of small or
poorly supported libraries proceeding with automation in
one form or another. One authority estimates that public
libraries can only afford 1-3 percent of their annual
budget for automation.[3] If that formula is applied to
the majority of public libraries, it represents only
$500-1,500 annually. That is an arbitrary formula, but
whatever is used as a basis for determination, it is
doubtful that many libraries can afford the cost of
purchasing the hardware and software, converting to a new
system, and then maintaining that system using their own
financial resources. The smaller the institution, the
greater the likelihood that automation will consume a large
percentage of the institution's operating budget.

4.1 Barriers to Cooperation

Despite the promise offered by cooperation, it may also
present some disadvantages. Cooperation is never without
additional costs. A library must invest time in

identifying common goals, creating an operational
framework, compromising on specifications, and apportioning
costs fairly. While small- and medium-sized public
libraries have the most to gain from cooperation, they are
also least likely to have the staff and time necessary to
allocate to cooperation. Most of their attention has to be
devoted to keeping the door open and marshaling full
resources to operate what is typically an inadequately
financed service unit.

In addition to the direct and indirect costs associated
with cooperation, there may be legal considerations which
would restrict a library from contracting with similar
institutions. These restrictions are rapidly disappearing
in state after state, but there are some instances of legal
barriers to certain actions which might be essential to
cooperation in automation, such as joint ownership of a
computer. Libraries planning to cooperate in the
application of automation should obtain an attorney's
opinion on these planned actions, based on local and state
statutes. A library board may require that a cooperative
agreement be reviewed by an attorney, and better assistance
can be provided if this individual is introduced to the
plan at an early stage. Cooperation in automation raises
some unusual legal questions, such as rights to a commonly
developed database, liability in the event of lost records,
and a host of arcane issues, which may not arise if the
library elects to automate unilaterally.

There are also psychological barriers to cooperation. A
great deal of lip service is given to sharing resources and
working together, but despite this, libraries are often
reluctant to cooperate. For one thing, local pride and
jealousies sometimes interfere. Adjoining towns may have
animosities which have evolved and been reinforced over
many years. Some libraries may feel reluctant to automate
jointly because they fear it will reduce their local
autonomy on policies. One library, for example, may feel
that its collection is superior to that of another library,
and creation of a joint circulation system might result in
the second community drawing upon the collection of the
first, rather than improving its own collection. Another
library system may take a strong stand against delinquent
borrowers, while yet another may be lenient. While it is
possible to design automated systems around differing

policies, every library believes its own practices are
usually best and should be applied universally. The
psychological barrier is a major one and should not be
ignored. Surmounting it takes a great deal of
statesmanship, patience, and tolerance.

Libraries may also have differing goals for automation.
One institution may feel that a circulation system is its
first priority, while another may believe online cataloging
is the first step. Reconciling these different goals, and
within them, differing priorities, will also require
negotiation. Although they share many common features,
public libraries are not identical. There is no typical
public library. Communities of similar size and wealth may
have traditions relative to their public libraries which
set them at opposite ends of the spectrum in many respects.

While a joint venture promises to reduce costs for
automation, it may actually increase some specific expenses
and make financing more difficult. For example, one
library can approach its taxing authority for financing for
the automation of a process more easily than if two
libraries approached two different taxing authorities with
a joint proposal. Complications can be anticipated as the
number of jurisdictions increases. Additional legal
opinions will probably be required. More time and expense
will have to be invested to explain and justify the
venture. More questions of ownership, liability, and
cancellation will arise.

Another complication may be presented by differing
standards. For example, one institution may feel that a
brief bibliographic record is sufficient for resource
sharing. Another may insist that only a full record should
be used. Again, it may be possible to accommodate varying
standards in certain applications of automation. However,
that may reduce the effectiveness of cooperation and
increase costs.

There are a host of real and imagined reasons why
automation should not be approached on a cooperative basis.
In the final analysis, if libraries elect not to implement
a project for any of those reasons, there is little that
can be done other than to point out that almost every

automated application has been successfully implemented in some part of the nation on a cooperative basis.

4.2 Advantages of Cooperative Approaches to Automation

The most obvious advantage of joining with other libraries is the chance to share the cost of purchasing; converting, creating, and maintaining data files; and maintaining automated equipment and procedures. Given the financial situation of many public libraries, this is often the only way they can consider automation. Administrators of several libraries that have automated their systems have reported that it has cost them as much to convert their manual systems as to purchase the hardware and software. They have also reported continuing expenses averaging between one quarter and one third of that purchase price to pay for ongoing computer and software maintenance and telecommunication charges.

These figures will differ from one application to another, and some libraries may experience more or less expense depending upon the approach they select in solving uniquely local problems. Nonetheless, the cost of purchasing an automated system is only a portion of the total expense the institution will face. Sharing this expense with other libraries spreads the risk and provides a better foundation for financing solutions to problems which may unexpectedly arise.

Cooperation may also allow libraries to take advantage of the economy of scale. For example, online circulation control usually requires the purchase and application of barcode or OCR (optical character recognition) labels, i.e., labels which can be used by some machine device to identify materials, on those items to be circulated using the system. There may be a significant reduction in price if the orders can be consolidated and quantities increased. The same advantage holds true for equipment. Thirty computer terminals will usually cost less per unit than fifteen. Computer storage capacity is often cheaper per unit stored on larger storage units. There are, however, disadvantages to offset these savings. For example, expensive telephone charges may be incurred when several libraries share a computer. A library which purchases its

own stand-alone system may have no telephone charges unless
it has a branch system. In general, though, there are more
advantages to joint purchase of a system because of the
potential for economies of scale.

Another factor supporting cooperation is the ability to
recruit more highly qualified personnel for the project.
Many commercially available systems are advertised in such
a fashion as to lead to the conclusion that they will
operate by themselves. Hence, they are often called
turnkey systems. There are few applications of automation,
however, that do not require some dedicated staff support.
Almost every application requires some conversion effort
and, consequently, staff time. Coordination is also
required.

If cooperative automation is undertaken, the participants
must apportion responsibilities for implementation,
conversion, and maintenance among themselves. It may be
possible to share the workload equally without temporary or
permanent additions to staff. More often, particularly
with more complex applications, such as online circulation
control, some additional personnel are required. The
pooled resources of the participating libraries increase
the likelihood that more highly qualified personnel can be
recruited. Greater specialization is possible in personnel
assignments, and duplication in training effort can be
reduced.

Another major justification for joint effort in automation
is the opportunity it provides for accessing more
resources. A single library that establishes an online
cataloging system is saving very little. Compare this
effort with that of the more than 3,500 libraries sharing
the use of the giant OCLC Online Union Catalog, and the
advantages of cooperative automation quickly become
apparent. Current estimates are that the average public
library finds a catalog record in the OCLC database about
94 percent of the time, thereby reducing original
cataloging to a minimal level.

The increased accessibility of holdings information also
offers more opportunity for interlibrary borrowing and
increased service to the public at substantially lower
cost. These same benefits are possible, on a diminished

basis, in cooperative use of online circulation systems. While it may be difficult to place a dollar value on accessibility, it represents a tangible benefit and a solid motivation for cooperation despite the existence of real and imagined barriers. Cooperation in the use of local resources blends well with state and national goals and objectives for libraries, which may not appear to be a significant benefit at first but may be a tangible one if the state library agency has provided financial incentives for joint use of newer technology. A number of states have done so and, despite present federal and state funding trends, it is likely that incentives in one form or another will exist to allow not only public but academic, school, and many special libraries to join together in applying newer technology to share resources at the local, state, and national level as networking capabilities improve. An individual library will not have the same opportunity to take advantage of these incentives as a cooperative group.

Finally, there are advantages in sharing experience. A cataloger using an online cataloging system can obtain training to effectively use that function. In time, that person will expand his/her capabilities. Several catalogers sharing the same terminal, however, can learn much faster by sharing their experiences. Some small libraries that share OCLC terminals have reported, for example, that periodic meetings to review techniques and problems have greatly increased their productivity. In some instances this opportunity to cooperate in the use of a system has allowed catalogers to specialize on a subject or format basis.

4.3 Cooperative Models

Libraries can adopt a variety of different methods to use automation. Two libraries may informally agree to share an online terminal for reference searching without any complicated agreement. While there certainly are many advantages to an informal approach to cooperative automation, it is usually wiser to develop an agreement in writing for any project with another library. It can be simple, consisting of a statement of purpose, an itemized list of what each participant will do as part of the agreement, and a list of mutual responsibilities.

The document should also state when the agreement begins
and ends and, if appropriate, a projected schedule of use.

For example, two libraries may want to establish a COM
(computer output microform) catalog of their holdings to
improve resource sharing. That statement could form the
first section of the agreement. One library could assume
responsibility for converting its bibliographic records to
machine-readable form and submitting them to the other
library at stated intervals and assume 50 percent of the
cost of producing the catalog. That would conclude the
second section of the agreement. The other library could
also agree to convert its bibliographic records to
machine-readable form, collect the records of the other
library, assume 50 percent of the cost of producing the
catalog, and assume responsibility for forwarding this data
to a vendor and handling the accounting. That statement
concludes the third part of the agreement. Finally, both
libraries could agree to continue the arrangement for a
specified period, spell out conditions for withdrawal, and
determine ownership of the joint database that will be
developed.

More complex projects clearly require a more detailed
contract. It will be wise to retain legal counsel for that
purpose, although one of the institutions may be able to
provide this service. The concept of equal or shared
responsibility is the essential element of this model.

Another variant would be to vest all responsibility in a
single library. For example, one library may lease online
cataloging services and provide those services for a
mutually determined sum to other libraries participating in
the project. This will impose a heavier workload and
responsibility on one institution, but it may be more
efficient than scheduling different hours when individual
libraries may use the terminal and having each library pay
the traveling expenses and assume the travel time for an
employee to visit the host library. Not all automated
applications lend themselves to this model, but many do.
Frequently the stimulus for such an arrangement comes from
a large urban public library that would like to spread the
costs for maintaining automated services by developing and
offering a contract service to suburban libraries.

A third model would be a nonprofit organization for the purpose of implementing a cooperative automation project. Such an organization might involve incorporation and creation of a set of bylaws and a governance structure. An independent staff and structure might be required. This model clearly is appropriate only for larger and more complex automation projects. It requires more legal work and more overhead but has several advantages. The organization may be used as a financing mechanism. An independent organization also reduces the liability of individual libraries if something should go wrong.

Still another model uses a third party (a network, another department or institution, or a service bureau) to assume administrative and coordinative responsibilities for automation. Many library cooperative systems or federations use this option. The staff of these systems assume responsibilities as neutral mediators in developing cooperative specifications for automation. They may possess the expertise to negotiate with the suppliers of computerized services, and they would be a logical place for staff to be housed to maintain the cooperatively operated automation system. Even though not all the libraries that may be members of the federation may elect to participate in the project, it would still be possible for a group of members to work through their federation as a framework for joint use of automated systems.

Other third parties that might be used would be the computer departments of nearby colleges or universities, local hospitals, or school systems. Some of these institutions may not want this responsibility, or they may place a large overhead expense on the service, thereby eliminating it as a feasible model. However, a third party may have surplus or underutilized computer capacity and staff time and this model may provide substantial savings to both it and the cooperating institutions.

Yet another option would be to contract with a commercial computer service bureau. These bureaus, based on shared use of computer equipment, exist to offer services to any organization. Typically, many small businesses and industries are customers because they have found it economically advantageous to purchase computerized services rather than create their own departments. That same logic

can be applied to cooperative purchase of computer services
by libraries. The service bureau may offer very economical
administrative services, such as payroll, because the
service bureau is likely to have software and other
services designed for such applications. Few service
bureaus have existing packages for libraries, but some may
be willing to create or adapt packages for such use.

4.4 Selecting the Best Model for Cooperation

There is no ideal model for cooperation. Individual
libraries must decide which model best suits the
application they wish to automate and which model gives
them the best quality service for the lowest cost. There
are guidelines, however, which will simplify the process.

It is not wise to decide upon a cooperative model before
the participating libraries have a plan for present and
future automation. It becomes cumbersome, as well as
expensive, to change cooperative mechanisms as the group
expands its use of newer technology. For example, a
service bureau may provide satisfactory cooperative payroll
services, but it is not a likely source for online
cataloging. Likewise, changing automated systems from one
vendor or plan to another requires rethinking, and
sometimes reconverting, the whole system. Just as an
individual library must develop a plan for automation
before it proceeds to implement individual projects, it is
even more important that cooperating libraries undertake
this same process. The plan should have a realistic scope
and assist the design of a cooperative model or framework
which is appropriate for the number of participants and
their needs.

Informal agreements may be used at the outset, but they
should be written to allow the transfer and evolution to a
large model as further automation is desired. There are
three other elements which should influence libraries in
deciding which model to employ for cooperative automation:
time, cost, and compromise.

The larger and more elaborate the model selected, the more
time required to implement it. If time is important to a
group of libraries, they should select a simple model--

perhaps just a cooperative agreement among themselves.
However, the smaller and simpler the cooperative framework,
the greater will be the likelihood that the participants
will have to assume a larger share of the costs and
responsibilities of the project. A contractual agreement
among four libraries to establish a COM catalog is likely
to be more economical than a COM project launched by one or
two libraries. However, costs may be reduced even further
if 16 libraries are involved in the effort and if each
elects to assume a proportional share of the work. The
larger and more elaborate the cooperative framework, the
greater will be the number and/or type of the compromises
that its participants will have to make. While many
applications of automation permit great flexibility, there
are different standards, as well as policies which do not
lend themselves to universal adoption.

4.5 Calculating the Cost of Cooperation

The preceding section of this chapter emphasized the
economic advantages of cooperation in the use of computers,
but such advantages may not accrue for every application
and for all sizes of libraries. Some institutions may well
be better off purchasing their own systems. In some
instances the time and effort devoted to establishing a
cooperative model for automation may be so great that they
outweigh the economic advantages.

There are an enormous number of options in automation and
cooperation with other libraries. The challenge is to
establish a formula which can be used by a library
administrator to weigh the relative advantages of
automating alone or joining with others. There are several
guidelines which can be applied.

First, in considering automation, it is wise for a library
to obtain an estimate for implementing an automated project
by itself as a basis for comparison with the cost estimate
for a cooperative project. While it is usually cheaper for
a group of libraries to automate, an individual estimate
provides objective data and is good business practice.

Second, calculate the time which may be required to develop
a cooperative plan for automation, the time that will be

required to establish a framework for implementing that plan, and the application identified as having the highest priority. Given the complexities of automation and cooperative agreements, this may be difficult, but it is an expense which must be considered and weighed. It might be well to propose that the libraries planning the effort establish a target date for reaching specific decisions and determine jointly the frequency and length of the meetings required to reach those decisions. This time factor will provide one means of estimating the cost of cooperation that can be converted into dollars.

Third, as the costs of a cooperative project are determined through preliminary proposals and conversations with vendors, separate those expenses which are specifically related to cooperation. For example, telecommunication costs are an expense necessary in the cooperative use of a computer. Also, the computer may require certain enhancements which would not be necessary if a single library used the system.

Adding the cost of a library's share of the computerized application, the pro rata share of maintaining it, together with the time required for reaching a cooperative agreement, and the additional hardware and software related expenses solely attributable to cooperative use, will provide a reasonable estimate of the true expense for the project and the cost or the benefits of cooperation. Those can be compared to the cost of individual purchase and maintenance of the system.

These guidelines are a simplified approach to what may be a complicated process. Cooperation requires personnel time. There are tangible advantages to cooperation, such as improved access to resources, but there may also be considerable expenses.

4.6 Summary

One of the critical decisions in automation is whether to proceed unilaterally or in cooperation with other libraries. There are many real and imagined barriers to cooperation. Among them are legal restrictions, potential loss of autonomy, psychological barriers, financial

complexities, differing goals and standards among the
participating libraries, and the probability that greater
time will be required to develop a cooperative project.
Despite those barriers there are many examples of proven
success in the cooperative adaptation of almost every form
of automation. There are tangible cost savings which can
be achieved cooperatively--some libraries could not afford
to use computers at all if it were not for cooperation.
The economies of scale may allow substantial savings in the
purchase of supplies, services, and equipment.

Another major advantage of cooperative automation is the
improved access to resources it provides. In addition,
libraries have the opportunity to recruit more highly
qualified personnel required to operate and maintain the
automated systems on a cooperative basis, and they can
share their experiences by automating cooperatively. State
and national priorities also stress cooperative use of
local resources and may provide tangible incentives to the
cooperative use of automation.

A variety of cooperative models exist. These include
simple agreements based on equal or shared assumption of
responsibilities among the participants; direct contract
with a single library that assumes full responsibility for
the effort; creation of a nonprofit organization or
corporation for this purpose; use of a third party, such as
a library federation, academic institution, hospital, or
school system computer department; and cooperatively
contracting with a service bureau.

Selection of the best cooperative model depends upon the
needs of the participants and the computerized application
they wish to implement. The participating libraries should
develop a cooperative plan for automation as a basis for
selecting a model appropriate for their present and future
needs. The participants should then consider time, cost,
and compromise in reaching their decision. Larger and more
complex cooperative models require more time and
necessitate more compromises, but smaller and simpler
models may represent greater cost and greater individual
responsibility.

Finally, estimating the cost of cooperation is difficult because of the variety of applications and models available. Nonetheless, the administrator should always obtain an estimate for individual automation as a basis for comparison with the cost of a cooperative project and should also consider the time required to arrive at a cooperative plan for automation, to develop a cooperative framework, and to implement the application of highest priority. Those additional expenses in hardware, software, operating personnel, and maintenance which can be isolated purely as expenses necessary for cooperation constitute the final component of the cost. Weighing those expenses against the cost of individually automating will give the administrator a basis for determining the cost of cooperation, but the cooperative model should also be considered in the context of certain advantages, such as increased accessibility to local resources.

5

Financing

Discussions with selected groups of public library
administrators from communities of all sizes reveal that
cost is one of the major barriers to the adoption of
automation, even when cooperation can be employed to reduce
the burden upon individual libraries. Costs can range from
as little as $500 for a very low-cost personal computer to
several millions of dollars for a turnkey system which can
incorporate all the services needed by a large library.
Sometimes the expenditure can be made out of existing
revenues; more often, the purchase of automated services or
applications requires a special approach. There are
several methods that can be employed.

5.1 Major Cost Elements

Some libraries look at automation as a one-time purchase.
It is true that the initial expenditure for equipment and
software, and for the facilities remodeling often required,
represents a significant figure, but other elements must
also be considered. Besides the initial purchase, there is
the cost of converting both records and materials to forms
which can be used by the system, the ongoing expense for
maintenance and operation, and finally, the need to
eventually replace that equipment. In some applications,
such as the purchase of online cataloging services or an
online reference service, these expenses may be bundled.
But in a large number of other applications they are not,
and the total of these expenses can equal or exceed the
initial purchase price.

The initial purchase expense and costs associated with
conversion to the new system normally represent a one-time
commitment. The equipment and software costs can be
obtained from the quotes or bids of the vendors. Costs for
converting both records and materials are more difficult to
obtain because of the various methods which can be used.
Often a vendor can provide an estimate; some vendors offer
a conversion service. One element occasionally forgotten
is training library staff to be able to use the new system.
Such training is an expense usually associated with
conversion and should be supplied by the vendor as part of
the purchase price for the equipment and software, but some
vendors may handle this separately. The following chapters
include guidelines that will help in estimating some
conversion costs.

Some administrators ignore the conversion process entirely
because they believe existing staff can absorb work for the
new application without requiring additional time or effort
other than some training. They reason that the automated
application will replace the current manual method and
provide their staff with more time to undertake any tasks
pertinent to conversion. Indeed, some simple applications
allow this. Other administrators, concluding that they
will have a difficult enough time gaining approval to
acquire hardware and software, decide against seeking
additional funds for the conversion effort. This is not
realistic. Conversion to a complex application, such as
online circulation or an online catalog, will place a
considerable burden upon staff and result in inconvenience
to the public if funds for the additional work hours and
staff required for conversion are not obtained.

Maintenance and operating expenses are ongoing costs which
must be determined before the institution decides to
automate. Both hardware and software require some
maintenance; even a small personal computer or a computer
terminal requires regular maintenance and occasional
repair. Every reputable vendor can provide estimates of
this expense. Data should be obtained as part of the
quotation or the bid on the purchase of the hardware and
software.

In addition, most types of automation will add some
personnel requirement, if only a realignment of duties.

Even a public service terminal will require staff attention because some patrons will not understand how to use it. Certain automated services, such as online cataloging, generally save personnel time in comparison to manual methods, and it is possible to calculate that saving if the library has sound knowledge of the present costs of its services and procedures. Often it does not; the next chapter will provide some guidelines for collecting this cost data.

Some automated services require special supplies, such as labels, computer forms, ribbons, and other miscellaneous materials. Costs for these can be significant. Online circulation control, for example, is likely to require replacement of all the borrowers' cards and overdue and reserve notices and allow numerous special management reports to be generated. One library converted to an online circulation system because it would allow prompt notice of overdues to its patrons but neglected to calculate the impact this would have upon postage. The manual system provided notice to patrons after two months, a point at which many patrons had returned their books. The automated system supplied notices after two weeks, resulting in a dramatic increase in postage for the institution.

Besides maintenance, operating personnel, supplies, and postage, the library should include telecommunication and insurance costs as part of its ongoing expenses for automation. Many automated applications require additional telephone lines and special communications equipment; that can be determined during the data-gathering process. Additional insurance expenses are almost always incurred unless the library self-insures, in which case additional money should be set aside for replacement of the hardware and software in case of accidental loss or damage, as well as for the conversion effort which would be required to restore the automated system. If the system does not have provision for storing or "backing up" the library's databases, then additional money should be set aside for reconstructing these databases. More will be said about backup methods in subsequent chapters, but it is always advisable to invest additional funds in hardware or software and in operating expense to ensure the database is protected, since that database is often the greatest investment in automation the library has made.

The cost of eventual replacement or upgrading of either the equipment or the entire system is often forgotten in calculating the costs of automation. However, it is doubtful that the application a library has adopted can be used forever. Calculating the cost for eventual replacement is also difficult, given the dynamic nature of the computer field. In some applications this is handled through phased upgrades of the hardware and software. Even this approach has its limitations, since the upgraded computer will eventually reach capacity or be superseded by another model.

In estimating the cost of eventual replacement, it is wise to ask vendors about their long-range plans for their products and services. They will probably be unable to provide cost estimates for their services or products beyond a five-year projection, but their intentions should indicate whether users will be required to convert to another manufacturer or shift to another state-of-the-art model. The cost for eventual replacement can be included as part of the library's ongoing budget or planned as a special appropriation or expense in the library's budget planning cycle, but it must be considered.

5.2 Outright Purchase

Library administrators often believe that purchasing a system is the only way to proceed with automation and, judging from discussions with selected administrators in various size communities, outright purchase is certainly common. The purchase advantages are: there are no long-term interest expenses, additional finance charges, or complications. Purchase also simplifies the competitive bidding process that many libraries are required to use. Outright purchase grants ownership to the library and may permit modifications to be made to the system to satisfy the needs of the institution. The equipment, and sometimes the software, may have a certain resale value when the library elects to upgrade, update, or even change its system.

Automation is likely to be one of the more expensive
investments a library can make. Usually only its building,
personnel, and collections will be more costly, and those
are paid for in an ongoing fashion. Therefore, if an
institution pays for its building and other major expenses
over an extended time period, it might be wise to consider
the same approach for automation. That way, the library
can get the hardware and software it really needs, rather
than having to make compromises because it has only a
limited sum for a one-time capital expenditure.

There are some disadvantages to outright purchase of
computers. For one, the library may make a substantial
investment in equipment which may already or soon be
obsolete. Change is so rapid in the computer field that
there is certain to be equipment with greater storage
capacity, more efficient operating processes, and greater
reliability just around the corner. The library may also
invest in a system which the manufacturer plans to pull off
the market in the near future, making maintenance difficult
and more expensive. Good planning and research, however,
should reduce the likelihood of purchasing obsolete
equipment.

More often than not, this decision will have to be made
based on the policies of the board and local government,
since adding yet another ongoing expense to the library
budget to pay off a computerized system may not be
desirable.

5.3 Lease

There was a period when the majority of computers used by
business and industry were leased. Maintenance costs were
part of the lease expense, and the hardware was regularly
turned back to the manufacturer and replaced with newer,
faster, more efficient products. Leasing also presented
significant tax advantages to business and
industry--advantages which do not apply to governmental
entities such as libraries.

Even so, there are many advantages to leasing certain
computerized applications. Leasing allows the library to
spread the cost of automation over a longer period. The

lease cost is definite and set for a specified time period, making budgeting easier.

If funds for the equipment purchase have to be based on property tax revenues, that may require an increase in the property owner's bill during the year the purchase is planned. Leasing, however, may require only a small increase spread over a longer timeframe and may consequently be more acceptable to taxpayers.

Depending upon the terms of the agreement, leasing could reduce the danger of obsolescence. If the lease is for a relatively short period, with an option to renew at a specified rate, the library has the chance to step out of the agreement and migrate to more efficient equipment or renew at a guaranteed rate. Depending upon who provides the lease, the library may have the benefit of the manufacturer's continuing support. If the firm that manufactures the product provides the lease, the firm is more likely to correct deficiencies discovered during the term of the lease, since it owns the product. On the other hand, if the lease is arranged by a third party, such as a bank or finance company, such a relationship may be nonexistent unless the manufacturer's support is spelled out in the contract.

A lease may be useful since it can be linked with additional requests for conversion and maintenance expenses, thereby serving as one justification for an increased operating budget. Usually the administrator is faced with substantial options in both the expense and method of implementing computerized applications. These options include partial lease and partial purchase. The vendor may propose sale of the computer and software, but lease of the computer terminals and telecommunications equipment, such as the modems (devices which are required for communications between the computer and terminals located off-site).

There are, however, a number of disadvantages to leasing. First, finance charges are included in the payment, and the interest rate may not be as favorable as the library could command in the normal money market. Governmental entities can usually obtain loans at interest rates far below prime market levels because the interest income of the lender is tax exempt. Some manufacturers or financing firms do not distinguish between lease plans for governmental and business customers. It may be cheaper for the library to borrow cash at a lower interest rate and buy the equipment, rather than lease.

Another major disadvantage to leasing is that the institution has no equity in the equipment. At the end of the lease period, it has only the service it has obtained. Some overhead expense must also be added to the cost of the lease. The exact amount is often difficult to determine unless it is spelled out in the contract. A business can normally deduct certain of these expenses and the interest from its taxes, but a library has no such advantage.

While a lease may give a library greater flexibility in changing equipment or services, that advantage depends upon the terms of the lease and the nature of the application. For example, if the lease binds the library for five years, then the institution has gained very little. It is taking the same risk as if it purchased the equipment, since five years is a typical lifetime for some computer applications. If the lease is for hardware or for an application which will not require expensive conversion, then the lease may be satisfactory. However, if the library has to construct a completely new database or go through other major changes if it elects to terminate its lease, then this option may be more expensive than other arrangements.

5.4 Lease-Purchase

To make leasing more attractive, many manufacturers offer a compromise between purchase and lease. The customer does not have to make a major budgetary commitment up front to get the equipment and has an opportunity to build equity in the equipment during the lease period. In some instances, the customer can terminate the lease and apply all or part of the lease payments toward the purchase of the hardware.

As with any compromise, lease-purchase has advantages and disadvantages. The library will still pay some financing and overhead charges. It will take some risk in committing itself to equipment which might be obsolete. It will face a commitment in its operating budget until such time as it

elects to purchase the hardware or migrate to another
system, but it does have the advantage of building equity,
depending upon the terms of the lease. There could be only
a nominal surrender amount if the equipment is purchased at
the end of the lease, or it could be substantial enough to
actually result in ownership of the equipment at the
conclusion of the lease. Of course, ownership at the end
of the lease may be of little value if the equipment has
become obsolete or the library has outgrown it by that
time. Lease-purchase does grant the library opportunity to
gauge the trends for a specific period, benefit from the
present level of the technology, and then reach a decision
on purchase after it has lived with the application for a
period beyond the initial break-in phase. It is a trial
marriage and it may be a good alternative for an
institution unable to marshal sufficient funds for
purchase, provided the terms of the lease are flexible,
involve low interest and overhead, and the application is
appropriate.

Computer terminals are often provided on a lease-purchase
basis since they are likely to be interchangeable for many
applications and are a type of equipment which is
undergoing dynamic change. Computer terminals continue to
become cheaper, smarter, and more reliable. They are also
prone to receive a lot of abuse, depending upon the
application, and short-term commitment may be appropriate,
with the equity being rolled over into the next available
model if the manufacturer offers that option. Nonetheless,
the library will pay for the flexibility which
lease-purchase offers.

5.5 Deciding between Lease and Purchase

As noted, the decision to lease or purchase is complicated
by the variety of both applications and plans which are
available. There are some general guidelines which will
aid the administrator in reaching a decision. The first
step is to obtain the purchase price for the entire package
as a basis for comparison. Many vendors offer both
purchase and lease options, so the administrator should be
able to obtain comparative prices.

The second step is to determine the interest rate and the overhead charges which are part of the lease agreement. Federal and state statutes require the vendor or financing agency to provide this information. The interest rate should be compared with the rate the library can normally command from lending institutions in its area. To obtain a quote from a lending institution, a loan amount and term for repayment must be supplied; it should be possible to provide these figures from the vendors' preliminary price quotations and the library's anticipated budget for the period.

A third step is to review with the library's legal counsel any restrictions on the institution relative to leasing and lease-purchase agreements, such as complications with formal bidding requirements. Most states do not have legal impediments to lease or lease-purchase arrangements, but since libraries have infrequently made use of this option there may be a barrier which would require legislative action.

Next, the administrator should review the terms of the agreement and measure the degree of flexibility it provides the institution. If it is a lease-purchase agreement, particular attention should be paid to the equity and surrender value of the agreement. There may also be a penalty clause for conversion. The sum of the payments over the lease period should be computed and compared to the cost of outright purchase or outright purchase and repayment based on financing arrangements the library can obtain through local lending institutions.

Finally, the administrator should assess whether the application lends itself to leasing or lease-purchase. If the library is making a long-term commitment to a major application, such as circulation control, it is unlikely to switch systems in a relatively brief period. The cost to reconvert and rebuild a database would prohibit this. In such circumstances a lease may be an expensive alternative for the library; either lease-purchase or outright purchase might be better. On the other hand, a simple application which does not require long-term commitment, such as a public service microcomputer, might be leased more economically.

5.6 Time Sharing

Time sharing is a form of joint financing not often
considered in the library field. Institutions such as
colleges, hospitals, or local government may gain favorable
financing on a particular piece of equipment and have
computer processing and storage capacity which they will
not be using for some time. Rather than let this excess
capability be wasted, the institution may be willing to
share the use of the computer with a library or a library
cooperative. There are a variety of alternatives, ranging
from joint ownership of the computer to a simple charge
with pro rata sharing of maintenance and operating
expenses. Time sharing will require the preparation of a
contractual agreement which details the mutual and
individual responsibilities of the partners.

One example of this approach is the circulation control
system used by the Long Beach (California) Public Library.
The police department in that city purchased two computers
for its communications system. One was used as a standby
to back up the other system in the event of a failure. The
Long Beach Public Library reached an agreement with the
police department which allowed the library to use the
standby computer for an online circulation system. While
the library may experience an occasional interruption in
service when the main computer is down, such interruptions
are infrequent, and the library has established procedures
which can accommodate them. The savings have been
significant, since the library did not have to purchase the
computer, and it shares the cost of maintaining the
hardware. Its principal expenses have been for the
library-specific software and print materials, which it
cannot share.

There are, however, some notable disadvantages to time
sharing. Depending upon the terms of the agreement, no
equity may be gained. If the computer is being financed
and paid for over time, the library may be paying interest
at an undesirable rate. Reaching an agreement on time
sharing may be a complex and time-consuming process. There
is also the possibility that the library will eventually be
forced out of the agreement as the host institution grows
into the computer and increases its applications. These
disadvantages, however, can also be viewed as advantages

for some libraries. In all probability, a larger
institution, particularly a governmental entity, can
command more attractive financing rates. Joint use of the
computer will also mean that another entity will be sharing
the risks in the use of the equipment. The library may
also find that the host either may outgrow the computer's
capacity or capabilities and make it available to the
library on a favorable basis or decide not to continue time
sharing. In this latter case, the library, now with
considerably more experience, may elect to purchase its own
hardware.

5.7 Funding Sources

Conversations with library administrators who have
automated one or more services during the past several
years indicate that funds have most frequently been derived
from current operating budgets, special appropriations from
local government, or special grants based on federal or
state allocations. The smaller the cost, the greater the
likelihood the funds came from the library's operating
budget.

One authority has suggested that libraries can allocate 1-3
percent of their annual budget for automation,[3] but there
is no evidence on which to base this. For comparison, 1
percent of the typical library's budget is spent for AV
materials.[1] The automation plan which an institution
develops should consider the amount it can afford to commit
from its operating budget and establish steps necessary to
gather additional funds from other sources to help finance
the automation plan.

If special appropriations are to be sought from local
government, such as the city or county, then the board and
administrator should ensure there is support for this
alternative. Libraries which are independent districts may
not have this option and may be required to approach their
electorate directly. While special grants, including
general revenue sharing, the Library Services and
Construction Act, and other state and federal programs,
have often provided the impetus for automation in many
libraries, these sources are rarely of the continuing
nature needed to support the maintenance and operating

costs of automation. These ongoing expenses must be part of the local library's operating budget.

As previously mentioned, a number of cost factors must be weighed when a library adopts automation. One-time grants or appropriations do not cover all of those costs. On occasion, libraries may also draw upon special reserve funds or contingency accounts to finance automation. This is a valid use of these funds, provided they are unrestricted. However, the library may already be using the interest or earnings from these accounts to supplement local tax funds. If the library is dependent upon those revenues, then it will be taking a dangerous step in cutting income to pay for a major capital item which will place an additional burden upon the institution through conversion and added operating expenses.

Finally, user fees are employed in some libraries to pay for part of the cost of automation. In addition, some libraries have installed coin-operated microcomputers for patron use. Typically, user fees are charged for computer connect time and communications costs for online reference service. Research studies have revealed that 75 percent of all public libraries providing this service to their public charge a fee. [4] It is not common, however, for these institutions to charge the patron for staff time or for the expense of the computer terminal and printers.

While a library could establish a series of fees to finance computerization, this may be seen as contrary to the principle of the free public library. If there is a trend, it is for libraries to finance the automation of routines and procedures which are basic to the operation of the library, such as circulation, cataloging, etc., out of grants, operating budgets, or special appropriations. Fees have been applied to those services which primarily benefit the individual. This has often been a means of rationing public use of the service rather than a financing mechanism.

5.8 Summary

Cost, which is among the greatest barriers to the adoption
of automation, includes four elements: initial purchase,
maintenance, replacement, and telecommunications costs.
The initial purchase of hardware and software and the cost
of conversion are one-time expenses. This latter element
is often forgotten by the administrator in seeking funds
for automation. Maintenance and operating expenses, as
well as the cost for eventual replacement, are vital
elements in automation projects. Maintenance agreements
for software and hardware, telecommunication and insurance
costs, and ongoing expenses for operating personnel and
supplies are all continuing charges which should not be
ignored in reaching a decision on automation.

Outright purchase is one of the more common means of
proceeding with automation because of the desire to avoid
finance charges and overhead, but there are some
disadvantages to this method. For example, the library
assumes the risk that the equipment may be obsolete or
quickly outgrown. Leasing hardware and software offers
libraries the opportunity to spread out the costs of
automating and assume less risk in committing major funds
on technology with a potential short life span. The
disadvantages of leasing are that the library will have to
assume financing and overhead expenses and that it will
gain no equity in the hardware over the period of its use.
The terms of the lease could also be so long that the
library could not take advantage of new developments in the
field.

Lease-purchase agreements offer an opportunity for
libraries to build equity and eventually acquire equipment
which they could never purchase through their operating
budget or a special appropriation. On the other hand, this
alternative still involves financing and overhead costs,
and the terms of the agreement may permit only a limited
surrender value to be gained at the end of the lease.
Also, the equipment may be obsolete by the time the library
gains title.

The best means of determining whether leasing or purchase
is better for an individual library or cooperative group is
to obtain the basic purchase price as a basis for
comparison. Second, determine the interest and overhead
costs for the lease agreement and compare that rate with
the interest rate which the library could obtain through
local financial institutions if it borrowed money to
purchase the equipment. Legal counsel should also be
consulted to determine if there are any barriers to the
library employing a lease or lease-purchase plan. Last,
the administrator should determine whether the application
lends itself to lease. If the application requires a
long-term commitment on the part of the institution,
perhaps direct purchase or lease-purchase would be best.

Since computer technology is changing so rapidly,
obsolescence is perhaps inevitable. The need to replace
and upgrade both hardware and software is equally
inevitable and should be considered regardless of the
manner in which the library acquires an automated system.

Time sharing is a form of joint financing which the library
may wish to consider. This could involve sharing a
computer with another institution, such as a college,
hospital, or city or county government, drawing upon the
more favorable financing terms which that larger entity may
be able to procure. Advantages of such an arrangement
include shared risk taking, better use of the computer and
personnel, and greater flexibility for the library in the
long term. Disadvantages include the possibility the
library may be forced out as the host institution expands
its applications. Additionally, extended time will be
required to obtain an operating and maintenance agreement.

Funds for the purchase or lease of automated services
typically come from the library's operating budget, special
appropriations, grants, special reserves, and/or user fees.
Care must be taken in using these funds to ensure that the
library will have sufficient revenues to convert and to
maintain and operate the system. Use of special
appropriations and grants creates added hazards, since they
do not usually provide additional funds for operating
purposes.

6

Determining Current Costs

This guide is intended to help administrators determine
costs for automation and aid them in planning for effective
use of automation. The administrator may need some help to
calculate current costs for various services and
procedures. Without knowing the expense of maintaining a
manual operation which the library is considering for
automation, the administrator cannot make a valid
comparison.

For example, except in the case of a very large public
library, automated circulation control will probably cost
more than a manual system. How much more will depend upon
the nature of the present system and the conversion,
implementation, and operating costs for the automated
system. Knowledge of the additional expense is essential
for the administrator to budget accurately. Unfortunately,
there is little in the literature to help the public
library administrator determine costs for even the most
common services, and there are no standard methods of
calculating these costs at the present time. While a
special task force of the Public Library Association will
be concentrating on this need in the near future, some
interim methods are needed. This chapter will suggest some
simple methods which can be used to determine current
operating costs.

While the costs of automation will be an important factor
in determining whether a process or service should be
automated, the library administrator should not forget that
there are many tangible benefits to be gained through

automation. These benefits include improved access, better
quality services, and improved management information to
ensure better use of the tax dollar. The last chapter in
this guide will review these benefits and provide some
suggestions on how these might be weighed in the
decision-making process.

6.1 Factors to Consider in Estimating Present Costs

One of the easiest ways to determine costs is to contact a
library that has arrived at cost estimates for its
individual procedures and services and adopt those.
Unfortunately, there are many different ways to perform any
library procedure or service, and there are differing
personnel pay scales, standards, and policies of service
which may render comparison meaningless.

For example, one library may have the same pay scale as
another institution, but may have more liberal leave
policies. Some studies have demonstrated that only 60
percent of an employee's total time on the job is devoted
to the work assignment. The balance is taken by training,
breaks, preparation, vacation, illness, and assorted other
activities which substantially erode the typical 35-40 hour
week substantially. It is complex and difficult to adjust
for these differences between libraries.

Time-and-motion studies have been used by some libraries to
scientifically identify the amount of time and expense
associated with certain activities. Such studies can
create problems of morale. Sometimes the initiation of a
work measurement study may result in substantial changes in
productivity on the part of the staff. In some instances,
libraries have used sampling techniques to reduce this
effect. Staff have been asked to record their output or
responsibilities in time blocks of 30 minutes or an hour at
different times in the day to arrive at a median which can
be used as a standard.

There are also a number of articles and texts which contain
standard times for specific functions. Unfortunately,
because of lack of standardization in performing services
from one library to another, these figures may not always
be applicable. It is easier to compare the cost of an

entire service or function rather than a partial function. Even if it would be possible to assemble the times for all the tasks necessary for a total procedure, libraries do not process all their materials in the same manner.

Using sampling, time-and-motion studies, or standard times, an administrator can derive total personnel costs for cataloging a book. However, none of these would be a valid means for calculating total costs for cataloging if the library purchased some of the more popular titles preprocessed from a vendor and only cataloged gifts and other materials which it could not purchase in preprocessed form. Therefore, it is preferable to look at the cost for an entire process, even when only a single portion of the work is being considered for automation. Thus, only the inputs and the outputs need to be identified and included in the formula. However, if a mixture of work processes exists, costs can be recalculated if a substantial change occurs in the method of processing work.

Cost analysis (and a related factor--the error rate) is also complicated by variations in quality standards. Not every library has the same standards. Some may provide only simplified cataloging and devote their attention to service and assistance over the circulation desk. Other libraries may invest heavily in full and detailed cataloging because they believe such cataloging is the best way to provide the public with good access to the collection. While it is possible to arrive at certain simple methods to calculate cost, it is much more difficult to measure quality. Administrators must recognize this limitation. Automation of a process may result in significant improvements in quality, but the difference in cost between the automated and the manual method may be considerable.

As mentioned, error rate is a factor related to quality. For example, two secretaries may have entirely different speeds in preparing letters but, although the output of one may be twice that of the other, the number of typographical errors may be four times as great for the faster typist. A cost can be associated with the error rate, but it may not always be possible to measure that error rate in certain manual and automated processes. For example, errors in online cataloging may not become apparent for months or years. Errors made by a file clerk in entering cards in a catalog may never be found and the associated book might just as well be lost. A 5 percent error rate is generally attributed to each manual operation. This is one reason efficiency experts direct their attention to reducing the number of manual steps in a procedure.

The number of service points a library must maintain will also affect costs. A library which must maintain circulation desks at two exits will report higher circulation expenses than a library with only one desk, whether the process is automated or manual. Either method may lend itself to centralization, although automation often enables a library to provide remote service more cheaply to multiple locations.

In comparing costs, the policies of a library may add significantly to the expense of an operation, whether it is manual or automated. For example, one library may mail the borrower card to each new patron to verify home address; another may rely upon personal identification to verify address. The latter library will report significantly lower registration expenses because it does not have to process the cards for mailing and pay postal costs.

These are only a few factors to consider in estimating costs for the library's present services and procedures. Automation may cost more because it has the capability to perform additional services which cannot be easily provided through the manual process. It may not always be possible to place a dollar value on these side benefits, and in some instances they may be products or benefits which are not essential to the library. Nonetheless, they should be weighed.

With all these caveats, the following method is proposed for estimating the costs of several manual services and processes which are most commonly automated.

6.2 Foundations for Calculating Process or Service Costs

First, the library must identify the total amount of staff
time which is devoted to a specific service or process
being considered for automation. In many libraries,
particularly small- and medium-sized institutions, certain
duties may be fragmented. Everyone may handle circulation
or reference in a small library where everything is handled
over one desk. Cataloging may be performed by three or
four persons as time permits. Under these circumstances,
it may be necessary to create a simple time sheet for a
week, broken into half-hour time slots. The staff should
simply note (through the use of some common codes) how much
of their week was devoted to certain common tasks. A
typical week should be selected, and the staff should be
informed that the purpose of the survey is to determine how
much time is being devoted to certain tasks as a basis for
cost estimation, not to determine individual productivity.
If there are no significant differences in salary, it may
even be possible to keep the record anonymous. However, if
a variety of different salaries are involved, then the
sheet must contain the person's name or a unique identifier
for that salary category. The figures should be tabulated
and converted to dollars and staff hours.

In calculating these costs, use the amounts the library has
budgeted for them on an annual basis. This will simplify
the calculation process and, more importantly, will provide
a final figure that is a unit cost per unit of time, which
can be used to determine the cost recovery or break-even
time when comparing the manual process to an automated one.

Besides determining the cost and the amount of time devoted
to certain tasks, the cost of fringe benefits must be
included. The cost of fringe benefits can be determined by
obtaining the total amount spent for insurance and other
benefits paid by the library and prorating that amount
based on the percentage of total staff time devoted to a
specific service or process. For example, if the time
sampling reveals that the equivalent of one staff member
out of a total staff of four is devoting full time to
cataloging, and all salaries are nearly equal, then 25

percent of the total amount paid for fringe benefits should be added to the salary of that full-time person. In the case of unequal salaries, the fringe benefits must be apportioned in the same ratio as that of the salaries involved. Again using the example of one staff member out of a total of four, but with that staff member earning double the total salaries of the other three, then 50 percent of the total amount of fringe benefits must be added.

Almost every library process or service involves some supplies. Whether those are borrowers' cards, transaction slips, or catalog cards, it should be possible to identify both the expense for those items and the volume of annual expenditures. On occasion, certain functions require contractual services. For example, photocharge circulation systems may involve contracts for periodically servicing the equipment and processing the film. The cost of those services should be added to the other costs involved to arrive at total cost. In some procedures, special equipment is required. If it is rented or may soon need to be replaced because of wear or obsolescence, that expense should also be added. Many cost analysis procedures use elaborate formulas for factoring the original purchase price of equipment. For the present purposes, this cost will not be included in this procedure.

Finally, there is the question of overhead--the cost of the library facilities devoted to a particular task--which may include utilities, space, management services, such as accounting and personnel, etc. This is the most difficult parameter to calculate, and there are many different methods of doing so. For this guide, overhead will not be included. Only when there are major expenses involved in overhead, such as rental of additional space for cataloging services, does it merit inclusion.

In summary, the components of cost are salaries and fringe benefits for personnel, supplies, contractual services, equipment (rental or replacement), and in some instances, overhead. To arrive at unit costs per year, the number of products which are processed is divided into the total cost. The resulting figure can be used as a basis for comparison. This translates into the following formula:

$$\frac{a+b+c+d+e+f}{X} = Y$$

where a = wages/salaries of personnel involved in X
      b = fringe benefits for a
      c = supplies for X
      d = contractual service for X
      e = equipment for X
      f = unusual overhead for X
      X = a defined function's total output
          (the number of products processed
          in the defined time period)
      Y = unit cost for X

This is a simplified method for calculating the costs of
specific services or procedures, and it may require
refinement for a large library, but it covers the primary
categories of expense. Personnel costs are typically the
largest component: 50-60 percent of the total budget goes
for wages, salaries, and benefits, and many of the routines
found in a typical public library are very labor intensive.

To illustrate how this formula can be applied, a number of
specific library functions will be examined.

6.3 Cataloging

There are many different ways in which the cataloging
process can be automated. Besides online cataloging, the
library may elect to produce a book catalog from
machine-readable bibliographic data, or a COM catalog, or
to convert to an online public access catalog. Before a
library administrator decides which method to employ, it is
essential to determine the library's present cataloging
costs.

First, the library should survey the working patterns of
all staff involved in any way with cataloging, from the
preparation of the catalog copy through the maintenance of
the card catalog. Prepare a simple time sheet with
half-hour time blocks. Ask the staff to record time spent
on cataloging or catalog maintenance during a typical week.

Collect the total hours and calculate hourly rates and, based on this data, determine the number of full-time equivalent staff (FTE) and associated personnel expenses.

Second, obtain the total expense for fringe benefits and, on a pro rata basis, calculate the total for fringe benefits for cataloging personnel. If 10 percent of the total staff eligible for fringe benefits is involved in the catalog process, then 10 percent of the fringe benefit expense is assignable to cataloging, assuming salaries are comparable. If salaries differ, prorate costs based on percentage of salary, i.e., if 10 percent of salaries are devoted to cataloging, allocate 10 percent of the fringe benefits.

In some libraries, calculating fringe benefits can be complex. The cost of benefits may increase proportionally with the salary of the employee. Some libraries do not provide any fringe benefits for part-time personnel. Other libraries may prorate fringe benefits, depending upon the number of hours the person works each week. If it is possible, the administrator should calculate exact costs for fringe benefits, particularly if the library has liberal policies and these figures are likely to be significant. In the context of this guide, however, a simple proportion is suggested as a practical alternative for the administrator.

The quantity of cards and other forms used in the cataloging process should be identified. Unit costs can be located in standard supply catalogs or from invoices. Invoices from the preceding year should indicate the volume of supplies consumed, provided it was a typical year. If not, then the volume of supplies consumed in the cataloging process during a typical week should be identified and used as a basis for projecting total annual cost.

The next major item to include is the cost of any commercially supplied cataloging. Some libraries purchase as many preprocessed books as possible from commercial or cooperative processing centers. Cataloging charges for these should be identifiable, unless they have been bundled into the price of the book or audiovisual material. Some libraries also buy catalog cards from commercial or cooperative sources and handle the other processing themselves. In short, if the library is acquiring cataloging information from any source other than its own staff, there will usually be an expense associated with that acquisition, and it should be added to the list of total expenses.

The administrator should also review the cataloging process with the staff and identify any special equipment which may be used which is not owned by the library or which may require replacement soon because of wear or growth in the cataloging volume. Service contracts for maintaining equipment solely or primarily used for cataloging should be added to the cost of the operation.

Overhead expenses of an unusual nature may also be considered. If some major or significant expense is solely attributable to cataloging, then it should be considered. The components of costs for cataloging, in summary, consist of wages, salaries, and fringe benefits assignable to cataloging personnel; supplies; contractual services; equipment and maintenance; and in some instances, overhead. Once those costs are tabulated, the administrator should divide that figure by the total number of units (books, AV, etc.) which have been cataloged either by the staff or from commercial or cooperative sources; this represents the per unit cataloging costs as a basis for comparison.

Using the proposed formula and supplying actual dollar values, a cost for cataloging might look something like:

a = $20,000 (wages/salaries of cataloging personnel)
b =   5,000 (fringe benefits for cataloging personnel)
c =   800 (supplies for cataloging personnel)
d =   1,400 (contractual service for cataloging)
e =   1,000 (equipment)
f =   0 (overhead)
X =   5,000 volumes/year   (total cataloging output)

$$\frac{a+b+c+d+e+f}{X} = \frac{28,200}{5,000} = \$5.64 \text{ per volume}$$

6.4 Circulation (and Patron Registration)

Although many libraries tend to divide registration and
circulation, they are integral functions. Some type of
registration process will be needed with any type of
circulation method; therefore, registration should be
included in calculating the costs of circulation. Again,
the largest category of expense is staff salaries and
wages, and a survey of all staff connected in any way with
the circulation and registration process should be
undertaken to determine total time devoted to this service.
Half-hour time blocks should be recorded, together with the
name and title of the staff member, to determine hourly
rates.

After the survey sheets are collected for a typical week,
the hours should be converted into full-time equivalent
(FTE) employees for each job title for ease in calculating
total personnel cost. Fringe benefit costs should be
calculated, again based on the percentage of total staff
time devoted to circulation and registration. Supplies,
which are consumed for circulation, should be identified,
and the volume and costs should be calculated based upon
invoices and current supply catalog prices. These supplies
may include registration forms, borrowers' cards, book
cards, transaction slips, overdue notices, and envelopes or
postcards. Postage is an important expense in the
circulation procedure and should be identified and
included. If the library does not keep separate records on
what percentage of its total postage goes for overdue and
reserve notices, a typical week should be selected and
costs tabulated for that period, then calculated for the
entire year.

The type of circulation system used by the library may also
have some expenses associated with it. A photocharge
system will have expenses for film processing and camera
maintenance. Some libraries use microfilm reader-printers
to produce overdue notices or delinquency records from
film. The cost for the supplies and maintenance agreements
for this equipment should be identified and included. The
cost of any maintenance agreements associated with any
other special equipment should be included. Include the
cost of purchasing the equipment only if it is nearing the
point where replacement will be required or additional

equipment must be purchased because of growth in use. In
the same fashion, the circulation system may require
typewriters or other office equipment. Include the
purchase price of these items only if more equipment will
be required or replacement will be needed in the near
future.

Some libraries may contract for certain services associated
with their circulation or registration process, and the
expense of these services should be included in total
costs. Some libraries have partially automated, to the
extent that listings of delinquent patrons may be produced
by computer, or the transaction cards employed in the
circulation procedure may be machine tabulated and a list
of exceptions printed for processing delinquencies. Other
libraries may have retained the services of a collection
bureau to recover long delinquent library resources. All
of these costs should be considered as part of the total
circulation and registration expense.

Once all these costs have been identified and calculated,
they can be added to determine the library's total expense
for circulation and registration for the library's fiscal
or calendar year. The total circulation for that same
period should be identified then divided into the total
expense figure to determine the cost per circulation. The
formula is:

$$\frac{a+b+c+d+e}{X} = Y$$

where a = total personnel costs for circulation and
          registration
      b = fringe benefits for the percentage of staff
          involved in the process
      c = supplies and postage for circulation and
          registration
      d = contractual services associated with these
          procedures
      e = equipment which is rented, needs
          replacement, or must be added in the near
          future
      X = total circulation for the calendar or fiscal
          year
      Y = cost per item circulated for one loan period

Applying the formula to an actual circulation situation
might look like this:

a = $24,000
b =   6,000
c =   1,000
d = 25,000
e =   1,000
X = 250,000 items per year

$$\frac{a+b+c+d+e}{X} = \frac{57,000}{250,000} = 0.228$$

or an approximate cost of $ 0.23 per circulation.

If any major overhead expenses can be attributed primarily
to the circulation and registration process, include them
as part of the expense. Normally, a percentage of every
library building is assigned to circulation and
registration services, but calculating this as part of the
cost of those services adds complexities to the formula.
Furthermore, this is a fixed expense, and these areas serve
a variety of other functions, such as a security monitoring
point for the collection, directional assistance, etc. For
this reason, they are not included in total cost.

Administrators should also carefully note the products
which are generated by the circulation and registration
process and the frequency of those products. For example,
if it is library policy to send only one reserve notice, or
two delinquency notices at two week intervals, that should
be noted, as should the number of registered borrowers.
These elements will be important in comparing the costs of
the manual procedure with those of an automated system.

It may also be possible for the library to segregate the
expenses associated with interlibrary loan. If
interlibrary loan costs are included in circulation, that
should be noted and the number of requests received and
sent should be identified. If the library is considering
an automated method to improve its interlibrary loan
services and wishes to determine present costs, it can use
the method just described to arrive at those figures. Many
automated activities, such as a shared online circulation

control system, will dramatically increase interlibrary
loan traffic because the automated system provides improved
accessibility to the collection. As interlibrary loan
traffic increases, the library may experience increased
costs associated with that service, even though the per
unit cost for interlibrary loan dramatically decreases.
Increasing public use of library resources, however, is
what the public library was created to achieve.

6.5 Acquisitions

Acquisitions is a complex process in many public libraries;
it is often integrated with accounting and cataloging
procedures. Because there are a number of automated
acquisitions systems available to libraries, it is likely
that a library administrator may need to determine present
costs for acquisitions as a basis of comparison. To
identify personnel costs associated with acquisitions,
again use the survey method. Staff should record the time
they devote to the process, using half-hour time blocks.

Selection of materials is considered by some to be part of
the acquisitions process. The time staff spend reviewing
current journals and examining recently published titles is
part of the total expense. Rarely does any automated
acquisitions process include selection. Whether the
library administrator includes or excludes selection in the
total acquisitions expenses should be noted. When the cost
of the automated acquisition system is determined, the same
procedure can be followed, making results comparable.

Verification of bibliographic information is also part of
the acquisitions process. This information may be captured
for use in the cataloging process. For this reason, the
administrator may wish to include or exclude this activity
as part of the total acquisitions expense. Whatever the
decision, it should be noted (as was selection) in the
calculations, so that the cost of the activity will be
included or excluded, as appropriate, in later cost
comparisons.

The more specific or detailed the activity or service, the
more specific the personnel survey form needs to be. If
the administrator wishes to exclude selection, but include

bibliographic verification as part of the costs associated
with acquisitions, the form should note those facts. After
the total time for acquisitions is determined and converted
to full-time equivalent (FTE) staff time and cost, the
fringe benefits can be calculated based on the percentage
of total staff time devoted to that activity. Supplies,
contractual services, equipment, and unusual overhead
associated with acquisitions can also be determined based
on the techniques previously described and a total expense
can be determined.

The cost per unit can be calculated based on several
alternatives. The administrator may divide the total cost
by either the total titles ordered or the total units
ordered. Since public libraries tend to order a number of
duplicate titles, given the nature of their service and
their collections, the per-unit cost may be substantially
lower than the per-title cost. The administrator can best
determine which alternative better suits the library's
needs in comparing costs against automated methods, but
that decision should be reflected in the calculation and
reported as either cost per title or cost per unit.

Another alternative is to segregate acquisitions costs for
audiovisual materials from books, since AV materials
usually represent a much smaller percentage of the
library's materials budget. Generally, it costs more to
order audiovisual materials because they require more
complex procedures than those for books. It also costs
more to store, i.e., shelve, and circulate them. It is
helpful if the separate costs associated with nonbook
resources are segregated in all cost categories.

Many of the automated acquisitions systems are designed to
accommodate any type of material. For these, the
administrator may not wish to go through the additional
effort of segregating book and nonbook acquisitions costs,
but if this decision is made, the distinction should
certainly be noted in the cost figures for future
reference, and the same distinction should be made in
calculating costs for the automated acquisitions system.

6.6 Serials

Determining costs in handling serials is also complex.
First, unlike cataloging or circulation procedures, serials
work is likely to be an irregular procedure among public
libraries. Selection and ordering are usually done once a
year, every other year, or, in some instances every three
years. Only the claim work, check-in, distribution, and
similar maintenance activities are regular in nature, but
they do not represent total personnel costs. In addition,
some libraries do not have a consistent policy in defining
the difference between a continuation and a serial. A
number of automated serials systems are available, and the
administrator who is considering automating this function
must consider present costs in handling serials as a basis
for decision making on an automated system.

The administrator or the team considering serials
automation should examine some of the more common systems
available and determine how they treat continuations and
serials. If there are no distinctions, then cost estimates
should include both serials and continuations.

A staff survey should be undertaken during a typical week
to determine ongoing staff time and costs for handling
serials and fringe benefits. If the staff is unsure of the
amount of time devoted to ordering or renewing serials, it
may also be necessary to select a percentage of the serials
list and sample the amount of time required for this
effort. If a library has 1,000 serials and continuations,
then the time required to process 50 orders or renewals
should be adequate to calculate total costs. If the
library has only 100 serials and continuations, the time it
requires to process 5 titles may not be sufficient to
arrive at a representative cost. Depending upon the
frequency of the ordering and renewal process, this
personnel expense, coupled with the fringe benefits, is
prorated over the appropriate period, i.e., so much per
year, and added to the ongoing costs for serials control.

The previously cited formula used to determine cataloging,
circulation, and acquisitions costs may then be used to
arrive at total cost. The critical elements are staff
wages, salaries, and fringe benefits; supplies; contractual
services; equipment and maintenance; and unusual overhead.

This can be divided by the total number of serial titles (and continuations if they are included) to arrive at a unit cost as a basis for comparison.

There will be some differences in unit costs among many public libraries because of the variation in publication frequencies for the serials in their holdings. A larger library may order more scholarly or scientific journals, many of which are issued quarterly or even less frequently. Since less staff time will be required to process and control receipt of these subscriptions, a larger library's costs per unit may be lower than those of a smaller library with a list of serials issued weekly and monthly. However, the effort required to refine the costs to account for these differences may not be worthwhile. If the library wishes to consider those differences in reaching a decision, it should tabulate the frequencies of the serials in its list and divide by the total number of titles in that list to arrive at an average frequency. If the list is extensive, the library should tabulate every fourth or fifth title and divide the total frequency by the size of the sampling to arrive at mean or average frequency.

6.7 Business Services

The wide variety of business services (including word processing, payroll, and accounting) which are used by a public library and the number of automated business applications available make cost comparisons especially difficult. What makes cost comparison so difficult is that one piece of hardware may offer a variety of functions through its software. The expense of performing the library's accounting manually is obviously not comparable to the cost of automated systems which can handle not only accounting, but personnel records, payroll, and word processing. Nonetheless, the isolation of costs in performing the library's business services is basic to reaching a decision on whether to maintain or replace a particular manual procedure.

An administrator who intends to automate a single business service should also identify any other functions that can be processed by the automated system under consideration and then define the costs of manually performing those services to obtain a better insight to total costs. Many businesses and industries have found that it is usually more economical and efficient to computerize all their business routines wherever possible because of the opportunity to spread the initial cost of the computer over more functions, as well as the desirability of integrating all their business services, particularly where common information or files are used.

A staff survey form can be used to identify ongoing personnel and fringe benefit expenses, once the administrator defines which tasks should be included and selects a specific time period which is representative of the normal year. Many business functions are irregular, and a longer sampling period may be required. For example, depending upon the library's policies, payroll may be monthly, biweekly, or weekly, and a survey of staff time during one week may not be sufficient. Similarly, additional payroll work is usually required at the beginning of each year to process income tax withholding statements. If staff performing business services which have irregular workloads are unable to identify the amount of time devoted to these efforts, some sampling may be required to establish satisfactory time estimates to be factored into total costs for that function.

Calculation of supply, contractual services, and equipment costs should be included in the same manner as the other library-related services and procedures. It may be more difficult to differentiate these costs because of the multiple uses that such supplies, services, and equipment receive. Unlike catalog or borrowers' cards, the paper consumed in performing various business services may also be used for public relations and general correspondence. It may be well to sample consumption of certain supplies during the period of the staff survey and project total costs on that basis.

Once total costs are calculated, divide the total by the number of products or units associated with that service to arrive at cost. For example, total payroll costs can be divided by the number of employees to arrive at per employee costs. Many banks and commercial service bureaus will usually provide estimates for handling a library's payroll on their computer based on the number of employees.

Other services, such as general accounting, may be more
difficult to cost on a unit basis. Total volume of
activity might be a more practical figure to use, although
some accounting services are billed on a per-check basis.
To determine the most useful figure in arriving at unit
costs for its business functions, the administrator should
become familiar with the automated business services to be
considered and then adopt the unit of measurement employed
in the specific service to determine the equivalent manual
unit cost.

6.8 Summary

Many factors should be considered in comparing manual with
automated procedures, and cost is certainly among the more
important. Automation in some instances will represent a
greater cost but may still be desirable because of improved
accessibility to resources and improved public service. To
reach a decision, however, the administrator must be able
to determine the present cost of a procedure or service to
compare the difference in costs between the present and the
proposed procedures.

Present costs for services might be obtained from other
libraries, but it is likely that differing salaries and
procedures may result in misleading conclusions. It is
also possible to rely upon time-and-motion studies or
tables containing standard times for certain functions.
Those are complex processes, however, and there are
possibilities that staff morale could be affected,
particularly if they believe their productivity is being
measured. It is recommended that the library administrator
not seek to identify the costs for individual procedures,
but wherever possible, determine the total cost of an
operation or service. This eliminates many of the
complexities in cost analysis and allows unit costs to be
calculated. It will also allow the total impact of a
library's policies, standards, and error factors to be
included in that cost.

While cost analysis is a very complex process, it is
recommended that the administrator apply a simple formula

as a foundation for decision making in automation.   One
such formula is:

$$\frac{a+b+c+d+e+f}{X} = Y$$

Where a = total personnel costs determined for
          the function
      b = fringe benefits for those persons
          involved in the function
      c = costs of supplies consumed in the
          procedure or service
      d = costs of contractual services involved
          in the procedure or service
      e = rental or replacement costs of equipment
          necessary for the procedure, or additional
          costs of equipment if more will be required
          in the future
      f = costs for any unusual overhead which might
          be solely attributable to the service or
          procedure
      X = total volume or output for that service
          or procedure (i.e., circulation if the
          cost of circulation procedures is
          being determined, etc.)
      Y = unit cost

Examples of how this formula can be used were included for
cataloging, circulation and registration, acquisitions,
serials, and business services. Personnel costs can be
determined by using a simple staff survey form for a
typical week, asking the staff to record their time in
half-hour time blocks. If the work being measured is
irregular in nature and a survey will only measure ongoing
expenses, it is proposed that a sample may be taken of the
time required to complete the work during the heaviest
period. This can become the basis for calculating total
personnel costs.

7

Estimating Automation Costs

Many different expenses can be encountered in automating various services and procedures and, depending upon the complexity of the application, calculating those expenses can be a difficult task requiring the efforts of a team of consultants. Although this guide will not provide an administrator with a comprehensive review of all the potential costs associated with all of the possible computer applications that can be employed by a public library, it does focus on identifying the major expenses and some of the general principles to consider in automation. This chapter will illustrate some of the more common applications.

If the library is considering a complex application which may require the investment of hundreds of thousands of dollars, or if the administrator does not feel comfortable in applying the guidelines which follow, then it may be a wise investment for the institution to retain the services of a special consultant. There are specialists listed in the common reference tools for consultant services. Many major accounting firms offer services of this type. While their staff may be unfamiliar with libraries, they will be expert in defining costs for computerized systems. It is also possible to review the professional literature and identify authors who have written frequently on the automation of the procedure or service being considered. They may have the capability and the time to serve as consultants. Many state library agencies maintain lists of consultants to complement their own staff skills, as do many of the larger public library systems. Some networks offer consulting services to both members and nonmembers, usually at a higher cost to nonmembers. A unit of local government, such as the city or county, may have retained data processing consultants in the past, and may offer a referral. Finally, the library might consider retaining the data processing director or similarly responsible person of another library that has automated the application being considered.

7.1 General Guidelines

Every administrator usually finds it necessary to calculate costs on a preliminary basis for almost every change being considered by the library. Part of his or her responsibility is to assess whether major changes in service or procedure fall within the general funding capability of the library as a basis for any recommendation to the library board or other governing body. Depending upon the complexity of the change, that preliminary estimate may require subsequent modification as more data are gathered; however, it will provide a foundation for planning.

The following components are usually considered part of the costs of many automation projects:

1. Decision-making expenses
2. Development of specifications and evaluation of proposals
3. Equipment or hardware costs
4. Software costs
5. Maintenance charges for hardware and software
6. Remodeling or provision of facilities, including electrical work, air conditioning, and humidity control
7. Furniture
8. Communications or telephone charges
9. Computer connect time or computerized services
10. Operating personnel
11. Insurance and archive or storage expenses
12. Conversion expenses, including training
13. Supplies, including documentation
14. Replacement costs

Not all applications will require all these expenses.
Furthermore, some computerized services are sold with some
of these costs included in the total price. Since these
expenses are common to many applications and are sometimes
omitted by administrators when costs are being calculated
on a preliminary basis, these elements can serve as a
checklist.

7.1.1 Decision-making Expenses

The time and effort required for decision making is often
not considered part of the process, and, in the following
sections, that time and effort and the associated expense
are omitted. Libraries should remember that planning may
involve travel to installations, telephone calls to vendors
and other libraries, and staff time for estimating the
value of the application relative to local services and
procedures. During this time, the administrator or staff
will be collecting information essential to the preparation
of proposals or specifications. In the event the decision
is made not to employ the application, then this expense
and time is usually charged off against planning or
administrative overhead. If the decision is reached to
proceed, it then becomes part of the expense associated
with the project.

7.1.2 Developing Specifications and Evaluating Proposals

Later in this chapter there will be a review of the process
of developing proposals and specifications, obviously a
critical component of the cost associated with many
automation projects. In some instances, the library may
have to retain an attorney to assist in preparing a
contract or hire a consultant to develop the technical
specifications and perhaps aid in evaluating bids or
proposals received from vendors. On occasion, vendors will
supply technical specifications, or they can be obtained
from other libraries that have automated this application.
There are hazards in using specifications supplied by a
vendor or borrowed from another library, but they may aid
the administrator in reducing some of the time required for
this step.

Specifications supplied by a vendor may be useful in
identifying critical components, but they must be modified
to ensure fair opportunity for other vendors to be
considered. Otherwise, the bidding process would be
biased, and the library could be subject to criticism (and
perhaps a lawsuit) for preparation of restrictive specifications. Specifications supplied by another library may
satisfy the requirements and needs of that library, but
they may not be completely suitable for an institution of a
different size. In addition, almost all libraries have
different internal procedures; therefore, specifications
borrowed from another library may require some adjustment.

7.1.3 Equipment or Hardware Costs

Equipment or hardware costs are often the only expense
considered when a library plans to automate. While they
represent a major expense, there are some applications or
services where there are no hardware expenses. Certainly
not every procedure which a library automates requires the
purchase of a computer. COM catalogs are one example. In
other instances, the price of the equipment is included in
a monthly or annual lease or service charge. Sometimes it
is difficult to identify the equipment cost, and vendors
may be reluctant to itemize the charges for several
reasons. Some vendors add a handling and profit expense
onto their cost for equipment required in a "packaged"
system. They may fear that a customer will compare the
cost of purchasing the hardware directly from the
manufacturer (assuming the customer can deal directly with
a manufacturer) with the cost of that same equipment in the
package and elect to buy only the software. In some
instances, that is a more economical alternative, although
some vendors may adjust the cost of the software upwards to
compensate for their loss of profit on the hardware. It is
generally desirable to direct the vendor of any packaged
system to segregate the cost of the hardware from other
costs, since that allows greater flexibility in evaluating
the proposal.

In the case of the large bibliographic cooperatives,
charges may be levied differently. For example, OCLC does
not charge for actual connect time to its cataloging
subsystem. Instead, it tabulates FTU (first time use)

charges the first time a library uses a record it did not
create to produce its local cataloging. In the case of
OCLC, libraries are likely to find 94 percent of the
records they need already in the database, so this too can
be a significant factor.

7.1.4 Software Costs

Software costs are also among the more common items
considered in the purchase of automation. Many automated
services do not have a software charge associated with
them. For example, the purchase of online cataloging may
not require the purchase of software. The cost for the
development of the original software is included in the
charges assessed the user.

Vendors price software in a variety of ways. In some
instances, they may only license the use of software for a
specific library or for a specific length of time. It is
often easy to duplicate computer software, although
copyright and proprietary information restrictions prohibit
doing so. The vendor may adopt a policy of never selling
the software because of the fear that a library may elect
to reproduce purchased software and become a competitor of
the firm. Software costs will include the expense for
writing and testing the program prior to sale. For that
reason, a program which has general application among a
large number of libraries will be less costly because of
the anticipated return the vendor projects.

In acquiring software, it is essential to determine whether
the vendor will test its operation on the computer the
library employs. In turnkey packaged systems, it is
customary for the vendor to do this, but that is not always
the case when hardware and software are acquired from
different sources. A vendor may advertise that its
software can be used on a particular model computer the
library owns or is planning to purchase. However, there
may have been some changes in the design of the hardware
which may render the software inoperable. Testing and
debugging the software can be expensive and could become a
substantial additional expense if it is not included in the
price of the software.

7.1.5 Hardware and Software Maintenance

Both the hardware and software can have maintenance
charges. Hardware requires continuing preventive
maintenance, just as a typewriter does. Hardware may be
susceptible to breakdown because of the nature of the
application. Computer printers, for example, can
experience mechanical failure. Even solid-state electronic
devices require some maintenance and repair. In some
respects, maintenance agreements are like insurance
policies. They ensure that the manufacturer will service
the hardware and supply replacement parts whenever
required. Often the library is given a choice as to the
amount of time the equipment will be down before a
repairman arrives, or the library may be offered service
during selected time periods. For example, the vendor may
offer service within 4, 12, or 24 hours of notice. The
time the library selects will depend upon how critical that
computerized application is to the library's services or
procedures. An online circulation control system would be
more critical, for example, than an automated business
application which is used once a week. In some instances,
the library might consider purchasing backup equipment,
such as spare computer terminals, which would allow use of
a less expensive maintenance agreement. The administrator
can better judge this need by asking the vendor to cite the
mean time between repair or replacement for the equipment
being considered and by consulting other institutions
already using the same or similar equipment.

Public libraries are also likely to experience higher
computer maintenance costs than a typical business because
most public libraries operate for more hours per week than
businesses do. Typically, maintenance agreements offered
by vendors are based on an eight-hour day, five days a
week. That may be satisfactory for some applications, but
it may not be appropriate for an application critical to
public service, such as online circulation control, unless
the library is willing to risk and tolerate an interruption
in service.

Backup systems represent another maintenance expense. This
expense can be avoided for some applications. In online
cataloging, the system may be inoperative during various
times. While that is an inconvenience, it is still

possible for many libraries to assign personnel to other
activities. With an automated circulation system, however,
it is not good public relations to tell the patron to come
back another day when the circulation system is working
again. An alternative system or procedure is required. It
may be possible to purchase some backup equipment from the
vendor, or some manual procedure may be necessary to
satisfy this need. In any case, there is an associated
expense.

Software maintenance charges exist in some applications to
cover various problems which may arise after the system is
operational. For example, repair of the hardware may
result in a change of parts which is incompatible with the
software. The vendor may discover that the software can be
improved through changes required by another customer, or
there may be some change in the library's policies or
procedures which require some modification in the computer
software. Software maintenance agreements rarely permit
major redesign of the software, but they do enable the
library to retain the ongoing services of the vendor to
ensure the system continues to function as it did when it
was purchased. Just as with hardware maintenance
agreements, they are insurance policies.

Some vendors continuously upgrade their software and issue
revisions to all their customers. They may or may not
include this service as part of their software maintenance
agreement. In many respects, this is a convenience
enabling the vendor to standardize software maintenance.
The library taking advantage of the upgradings will assure
the application is state of the art, avoiding rapid
obsolescence.

The important thing in software maintenance agreements is
to determine exactly what is included. The library may be
guaranteed service in a specified amount of time but, if
maintenance cannot be performed off site, the library may
be required to assume travel expenses and overhead.
Software maintenance may have the same options in terms of
hours and days as hardware maintenance agreements. It is
the responsibility of the administrator to determine how
much delay in repair can be tolerated.

Any software maintenance agreement also needs to ensure close cooperation between the hardware and the software firms, if they are separate. If such cooperation does not occur, it is likely that the library will be mediating between both vendors, each claiming the breakdown is the fault of the other. This is one reason why there are inherent advantages in purchasing or leasing both the hardware and software from the same firm.

There are exceptions, but discussions with a wide sampling of library administrators support the assumption that maintenance charges for hardware tend to be substantial, while software charges are comparatively low. The rule of thumb is that hardware maintenance charges on a system, such as online circulation, may run between 25 and 33 percent of the original purchase price of the hardware per year, while the cost for software maintenance for a system representing a half-million dollar expenditure is likely to be $1,000-2,000 per year. In many automated applications, the software or hardware maintenance costs may be bundled into an all-inclusive service charge.

7.1.6 Remodeling Facilities

The remodeling of facilities to accommodate automation may cost little or as much as hundreds of thousands of dollars, but it is an expense which should never be ignored. A typical computer terminal may only require an electrical outlet to function if the application is written into the intelligence in the terminal; however, if the library does not have an electrical outlet where the terminal is to be located, an electrician's services will be required. If the computer terminal is one which requires a separate line from the main power panel to reduce line interference, installation could be expensive.

If the computer terminal is relatively "dumb" (i.e., has a very limited internal memory) and requires direct wiring to a computer in the library or connection via telephone lines to another computer located off-site, the cost of cabling to the computer is another expense. If the terminal is designed for dial-up access to a computer using standard telephone lines, and a telephone and an electrical outlet are near the location where the terminal will be placed, there may be no added expense. If that telephone must be reserved for other uses, such as public reference service, then the library will have to pay for the installation of another telephone. There may also be a problem if the library has all incoming phone lines going through a switchboard, since this arrangement is usually not suitable for computer terminals.

At the other end of the spectrum, where a library is purchasing a full computer system, the computer may require air conditioning, humidity control, and special raised flooring to allow cables underneath. Insurance firms may require installation of freon fire control systems, and special alarm systems may be desirable to protect the equipment in the event the air conditioning systems fail and the room overheats. The library may be so dependent upon the equipment that backup power generators may be needed to ensure the system continues to operate in the event of a power failure. Facilities remodeling can become an expensive component of the cost for automation.

In determining the expense involved in facilities remodeling, the administrator should examine both the library and the application. The vendor will be able to furnish information on the environmental and power requirements for the application. Many of the package systems do not require air conditioning or special power lines and cabling. Many modern libraries are constructed with ample power and communications outlets, particularly near public service points, but there may be flaws in even the best designs because of the relatively rapid changes in the technology. For example, the card catalog area may not have been designed with sufficient electrical or communications outlets for COM catalog readers or online public catalogs. Lighting may also be a problem, since somewhat different lighting is required for optimum viewing of a video display versus a card catalog. For large, multi-branch public library systems, rewiring of public service areas can easily be as great an expense as the cost of the hardware. Similar problems may apply to telephone lines.

If the library employs maintenance staff qualified to undertake this type of remodeling, they should be able to supply estimates of time and materials required. In most

instances, however, the administrator will have to obtain
estimates from an independent contractor or a city or
county electrical or maintenance department, as well as
from the telephone company. Design of a computer room, of
course, may involve retaining an architect and/or engineer
to provide cost estimates.

7.1.7 Furniture

Another component of expenses is furniture. It is possible
that existing table or counter space can be used, and no
added expense will be involved. Most libraries install
cataloging terminals on desks which formerly held the
typewriters that were replaced by the automated application. The administrator will have to evaluate present
equipment to determine its suitability for the new service
or procedure. COM catalog readers or online public catalog
terminals could be placed on top of existing low card
catalogs or counter-high reference shelving if they are
sufficiently sturdy. However, if the card catalogs are
being replaced, or if the shelving is heavily used, then
separate furniture will have to be purchased or
constructed.

Many library equipment manufacturers are redesigning their
lines to accommodate these requirements, and many office
equipment manufacturers have long offered furnishings
designed for use with computers and terminals, so it should
not be necessary to have custom-built cabinetry.

7.1.8 Communications Costs

Many online applications have communications or telephone
expenses. If several sites must be interconnected to share
use of a central computer, the library will have to pay
line charges. Additionally, it will have to either lease
or purchase modems to convert the messages to a form which
can be transmitted over the lines (unless these devices are
already built into the terminals). If these are local
lines, the expense may be relatively small, but if long
distances are involved, the cost can be substantial.

There are various methods to reduce these expenses. The major brokers of computer databases, such as System Development Corporation and Lockheed, allow access to their files through special value-added telephone networks which significantly reduce costs. Two of the more common networks are Tymnet and Telenet. There are also special hardware and telephone network designs which will reduce this expense.

Determining whether to use a desired computer application online or on a dial-up basis is one of the more difficult areas of cost estimation. If the library is online to an off-site computer, it may be leasing a dedicated telephone line, which is likely to be considerably more expensive than accessing the computer over standard or specially leased telephone lines only when the library needed to use the system. The online cataloging services of the major bibliographic networks, such as OCLC, are available either online or via dial-up to meet the particular budgetary requirements or volume needs of their members. Because of the size of these bibliographic networks and their capability to spread the telephone line charges among many members, there is a point at which it becomes more economical for a library to go to a dedicated line, rather than use dial-up. Once the volume of cataloging and other uses of such a system (e.g., acquisitions, interlibrary loan, and reference verification) reach a specific level, the telephone costs via dial-up and the inconvenience this process represents to its users dictate the lease of a permanent line.

Some computerized services are limited by the number of dial-up ports that permit access by users, and the lease of a permanent line provides greater certainty the service will be available when it is needed. The application will also dictate whether dial-up or online connection with the computer is required. Circulation systems are used frequently enough to demand online access. Reference services are less frequent, making dial-up access a reasonable choice.

7.1.9 Computer Connect Charges

Certain computerized applications (i.e., reference
services) have different charges, such as computer connect
time. The large database brokers, such as BRS, SDC, and
Lockheed, may require an annual charge, but the real
expense is likely to be the time involved in using their
databases. Each database has a fixed charge per minute,
and the computer will tabulate a bill for the library based
on the number of minutes its staff were connected to the
computer in searching a specific database.

In the case of the large bibliographic cooperatives,
charges may be levied differently. For example, OCLC does
not charge for actual connect time to its cataloging
subsystem. Instead, it tabulates FTU (first time use)
charges the first time a library uses a record it did not
create to produce its local cataloging. Whatever the
charge is called, estimating the library's expense for the
service requires determining the volume of use and the unit
rate.

7.1.10 Operating Personnel

Operating personnel may be required in some computerized
applications. Many times, current staff involved in a
manual operation are simply shifted to the automated
procedure, and no additional personnel are involved.
Online cataloging is an example of this. In other
applications, staff may have to be assigned to perform
certain activities pertinent to the operation of the
system. For example, online circulation control systems
require some personnel to start up the computer and turn it
off each day. There are often complex procedures
associated with this, such as recording the day's
transactions (known as backing up the system) to ensure
that records are not lost in the event of equipment
breakdown. In certain systems, records in the computer
memory are lost if the power fails. Many computer systems,
therefore, have hardware and procedures to preserve this
valuable information. In other instances, there are
procedures, such as the production of overdue notices,
reserves, statistical reports, and sundry other tasks,
which must be performed by specially trained personnel.

Not every computerized application involves this effort, and in some cases existing personnel can be employed on a part-time basis for this function, depending upon the requirements of the system. The administrator will have to determine operating personnel requirements and ascertain whether it will be necessary to dedicate full-time staff to the task. Frequently, an application will save staff time, thereby allowing retraining of a staff member for operating purposes.

Even an application which may not require an operator can consume some staff time in demonstrating how the system works or in aiding the public to use it. A good example of this is the COM catalog. Normally, the production of the catalog is done by a vendor, and the library has no need to retain staff to maintain and operate a computer. However, public service staff may be required to help patrons understand how to use the COM catalog and the microfilm readers. Good public information programs and directional information will reduce this requirement, but some staff time is required to develop the signage or educational materials for this application. Estimates for this time can be based on vendor information or the experience of other libraries that have adopted the application under consideration, but the administrator will need to modify that information based on the policies and practices in his or her library.

7.1.11 Insurance and Storage

Insurance costs should be considered because of the need to protect the library from the risk of losing a major investment. It is not only the hardware and software which require protection, but also the files, which are frequently the most valuable component. It should be a practice of the library to back up the files at periodic intervals to ensure that no data are lost. Expenses should be calculated for the archival or storage cost for these files. Most frequently, the files are stored on computer tape. There are various commercial services which handle automatic pickup and delivery. Often a library will recycle tapes, keeping the most current tape in archival storage and reusing the older tape for the next backup procedure. The library may elect to avoid part of this expense.

If it does, it should not keep the archival tape in the
same location as the computer because of the risk that both
the records and the computer could be lost in the same fire
or other damaging event. An insurance company and archival
storage firm can supply the administrator with cost
estimates for these expenses which, while they are likely
to be relatively minor for small applications of
automation, can represent significant ongoing expenditures
for larger installations.

7.1.12 Conversion and Training

Conversion expenses can equal the cost of hardware and
software in some applications. Shifting from one business
system to another may only represent a change in a few
procedures. On the other hand, a change from manual
circulation to automated online circulation control will
almost always require taking an inventory, reregistering
borrowers, building a database of the library's holdings in
machine-readable form, and a host of other steps which
could occupy a major portion of the staff's time for up to
a year or more.

Training is a component of conversion, as well as an
ongoing process, and is often bundled in the cost of
purchasing an automated application. The vendor realizes
that the library staff will not be able to benefit from the
application until they have mastered the commands necessary
to access the database and perform certain functions.
Sometimes the vendor will provide training not only for the
use of a packaged system, but also in the routines
necessary to convert to the system.

In estimating costs, the administrator must determine the
extent of the conversion effort and the training needed.
He may acquire information from the vendor and other
libraries. Online reference service is an application
where relatively little is required in terms of conversion,
but training is a considerable expense which will continue
as long as the library offers this service. Each new
database will require learning by the staff involved with
the service, or the result will be poor service to the
public and higher expense in computer connect time and
telecommunications charges.

Estimation of conversion costs can also be handled on a
sampling basis. Once the procedures are defined for
conversion, preferably involving the staff who will be
involved in the conversion, the administrator may conduct
rough sampling of representative groups to identify the
unit times and costs. Those unit times would then be
multiplied by the number of items to be converted. For
example, in online circulation control, tests may be
conducted in entering information on holdings and patrons
and in labeling materials, since those are major components
in the conversion to that system.

Conversion estimates will also be valuable in determining
whether the library should undertake this process
internally or contract for it. If additional staff are
required because present workloads are too high, then
sampling will be useful as a means of calculating the
number of personnel required and the amount of time it will
take to complete the task.

Some commercial service bureaus will undertake the
conversion of certain manual files into machine-readable
form. Other firms specialize in providing temporary
personnel skilled in clerical routines. Quotations can be
obtained from these firms based on clear specifications
provided by the administrator.

Some vendors and cooperatives also offer services which are
useful in conversion. OCLC and AMIGOS (an OCLC network
affiliate) offer a complete retrospective conversion
service. The bibliographic records of a library can be
converted to machine-readable form and sent to the library
for input into COM, online catalog, circulation control
systems, etc. Because vendors are familiar with how the
data will be used, they can generally do a better job in
converting the library's records than can an independent
service bureau. There may be differences in cost, however,
which will outweigh those advantages.

7.1.13 Supplies and Documentation

The administrator will also have to identify the special
supplies which will be required for the application and
determine unit costs. Some vendors furnish supplies as
part of their system; in other instances, the library may
need to design special forms. Many computer forms cost
more than those required for manual procedures because they
are continuous forms and require special edges for rapid
feeding into the printers. Some printers require special
papers.

If the administrator can use existing forms or join with
other libraries in sharing in the expense of a common form,
costs can be significantly reduced. For example, it may be
possible to simply apply a coded label onto existing
borrowers' cards, rather than purchase new cards.
Designing forms so that they can be used by a group of
libraries will increase the savings.

It is also possible to use the system to avoid paper. For
example, some libraries using circulation control systems
no longer print statistics on usage for individual
libraries, since that information can be accessed online by
any library interested in that data.

The computer or terminal may consume certain supplies which
are unique, such as ribbons or ink. Computerized reports
or forms may require special binders and storage equipment.
Automation holds both promise and danger in terms of
expenses for supplies. While computerized procedures
permit storage of data in much more economical fashion,
they also permit the proliferation of myriads of special
reports. The administrator will have to carefully weigh
the relative advantages of these reports and their impact
upon the budget for supplies, as well as the time it will
take to produce and digest the information reported.

Training manuals are a form of supplies, and they can be a
significant expense. Online reference service requires the
purchase of training and reference manuals for the various
databases for staff to become proficient in the use of
those databases. Applications where there is a high
turnover in personnel, such as circulation control, may
require a large number of training manuals.

If the system is undergoing continual change, and the manuals are not in looseleaf form to permit easy update, there may be a continuous reprinting of these manuals. Again, this can be avoided if the application is designed with enough online information for its users to avoid the need for paper guides. Some packaged systems are designed with special tutorial features or prompts which allow the user to learn the system with relatively little formal instruction. Other systems are complex and require considerable preparation before undertaking searches.

In estimating the supplies required for a particular application, the administrator needs to carefully review the forms and other supplies identified by the vendor or manufacturer, examine the application in other libraries wherever possible, review the local library's policies and procedures, which may dictate other special reports or forms, and then calculate total costs based on volume and unit costs.

7.1.14 Replacement Costs

Replacement costs were mentioned previously. They are hard to calculate and frequently ignored. One critical element influencing these costs is the life of the system. System life has been variously described as the amount of time it takes before the library outgrows the system, or until it becomes technologically obsolete and is superseded by another model, or the time it takes for the system to return its cost to the library in various savings or improved services. Some automated systems may never require replacement, but that is unusual. The technology is so dynamic that there is almost always a better product around the corner. It is possible to ignore replacement cost and ask the governing authority or the electorate for another special appropriation when replacement is required. It is unwise to assume the library could get along by returning to a manual procedure if an automated system it has employed for a number of years cannot be replaced. Wherever possible, the administrator should project future costs for replacement of the system and budget for this in gradual steps annually or incorporate replacement costs for automation in long-term capital improvement plans.

An alternative to replacement is periodic upgrading of the
system to satisfy the library's need for growth. It should
be possible to obtain information from the manufacturer or
vendor to determine what phased upgradings or improvements
will cost. Upgrading is another way to delay, postpone, or
plan for replacement.

7.2 Sources of Cost Information

So far, vendors or other libraries have been mentioned as
major sources of cost data. Preliminary cost information
can be obtained from firms that specialize in software
design and from manufacturers. Since suppliers of hardware
or software recognize they may be involved in a public
bidding procedure and the information they provide may
become public knowledge, any preliminary quote is likely to
be conservative. Furthermore, the vendor is likely to have
access to only limited information about the library and
its volume or activity. The vendor is likely to base the
quote on experience with libraries of similar size. Thus,
if any special requirements are sought, the administrator
should allow for this in modifying the preliminary price
cited by the vendor.

While this chapter primarily considers the estimation of
preliminary costs in automation, it also briefly discusses
the process of obtaining firm figures, and what to do if
there are significant differences between preliminary and
final costs. There are two primary methods for the library
to collect actual costs for automation, and these are often
specified by statute or local ordinance.

7.2.1 Request for Proposal (RFP)

The first method is the RFP or request for proposals. This
is a description of a general or specific problem coupled
with an invitation for qualified vendors to submit a
detailed solution with costs. The intent is to allow
vendors more flexibility in proposing solutions to meet the
library's needs. It is particularly valuable in more
complex applications of computer technology, where the
library may not have the technical expertise

to specify exact requirements, or where there may be many
alternative solutions.

The basic components of an RFP are:

1. A clear description of the need or problem
2. Details on the volume of activity appropriate to
   that need or problem
3. Any standards which are appropriate and conditions
   for acceptance (performance, reliability, etc.)
4. The type of information the proposal must
   contain and the sequence or format in which
   it must be presented
5. Information on how the price is to be quoted

One of the more common complaints received from vendors is
that RFPs frequently do not clearly state what is needed.
In some instances, it appears the library is confused by
automation and is unclear about its needs. If the library
has effectively planned for the use of automation and
studied the applications, that should not occur.

The RFP must also state both the volume of activity the
library experiences at present and that it anticipates in
the future. This will allow the vendor to determine the
size of the system required. The vendor must have
information about current and projected circulation,
holdings, registration, and the number of agencies served,
among other factors, to accurately estimate the cost for a
proposed online circulation system.

There are certain standards of performance the
administrator and staff should settle upon; these should be
stated in the RFP as items which are not negotiable. For
example, it may be decided that the online system should
permit entry of a patron name of indefinite length or that
the bibliographic record should be the full MARC record.
If the vendor wishes to submit a proposal, these standards
will have to be met unless the vendor wants to risk
submitting an exception which may result in a
disqualification.

It is also wise to specify the overall sequence and format respondents should use in their proposals. If the responses are similar in format and sequence, it will be easier for the administrator or evaluator to compare the substance of the proposals.

Finally, the RFP should always tell the vendor how, when, and where in the proposal the price should be quoted. For example, the library will usually benefit by having the hardware and software costs quoted separately. The same is true of hardware and software maintenance costs, since this will allow the library flexibility in determining whether to purchase the hardware and software separately.

7.2.2 Formal Purchase Contract

RFPs and formal purchase contracts are often used interchangeably; they do have commonalities. The primary difference is that the RFP usually requires the vendor to prepare the specifications for a solution to a problem or need defined by the library. In some instances, however, the library knows the solution it wants to use and has sufficient skill to prepare detailed specifications. The formal purchase contract usually contains the following elements:

1. Instructions to bidders
2. Contract
3. Specifications
4. Bid and bond forms

Some of these are common to the RFP, and some libraries may blend the two, depending upon local practice. Instructions to bidders tell the vendor when the bid is due, how it is to be supplied, where it goes, and other details essential to the process of submission. Frequently the instructions will tell the vendor how the bids will be evaluated. The contract will spell out the requirements upon the vendor in terms of completing the project. Mention may be made of penalty clauses in the event of delay or unsatisfactory work. Terms of acceptance and payment will usually be contained in this section. The contract will usually identify the detailed specifications which follow as part of the contract.

These detailed specifications will be produced by the administrator and/or the staff as a result of their research into the requirements of the library. Some specifications may be functional, where detailed steps are included. In other instances, a specification may be comparative. A specific model and manufacturer may be cited, and the vendors will be directed to supply that product "or equal." This is less common in library automation specifications, but the administrator can specify in the document a particular product which appears to satisfy the library's requirements. For example, a specific computer terminal may be identified as having the keyboard or other technical capabilities which are desired.

Bidding and bonding requirements are also part of this document. It is customary on more complex projects to require a performance bond to ensure that, if the vendor is unable to complete the contract, the library is compensated for any damages it may incur in the completion of the project. The bond is usually in the full amount of the contract, and there is often a bid bond, in a smaller amount, which is required of the vendor to ensure that only serious proposals are submitted and that the vendor is committed to the proposal if it is accepted.

Whatever form of proposal the library employs, it is customary for the document to state somewhere that "the library reserves the right to reject any or all proposals and to waive any irregularities." Inclusion of this, or a similar phrase, assures that the library is not bound to accept a proposal if the bids exceed the original estimate by a significant amount or if, for any reason, it lacks sufficient financing to implement the project. Furthermore, the clause also allows the library to accept a proposal which may not satisfy all of the requirements contained in the specifications.

We have covered some of the elements common to estimating the costs of automation, briefly touched upon the sources for this information, and noted the steps which will take the library past the preliminary cost estimation stage. To illustrate how these apply, a number of common computer applications will be reviewed in the balance of this chapter.

7.3 Online Cataloging

The most common approach libraries have taken to gain
online cataloging is to join or contract with one of the
regional networks or the major bibliographic cooperatives.
This approach is the basis for the following guide to
estimating cataloging costs. It is possible for a library
to create its own online cataloging system, but the
expenses for hardware and software are so great that this
is beyond the reach of all but the very largest libraries.
The largest bibliographic cooperative, OCLC, offers its
services through regional or state-based networks. The
library can obtain price quotes from those sources.

Cost elements associated with online cataloging are:

1. Profiling expenses
2. Hardware
3. Maintenance
4. Computer service charges
5. Communications
6. Training and documentation
7. Supplies and products
8. Conversion
9. Retrospective conversion

7.3.1 Profiling

Costs are associated with profiling, a method of
determining the format of cards generated by online
cataloging. These are one-time expenses and are usually
nominal, but they should be identified by the library and
calculated into the total costs.

7.3.2 Hardware

Hardware expenses associated with online cataloging include
the computer terminal and the modem. The library may also
elect to lease or purchase a printer to generate labels or
printed cataloging copy to be used in the editing process.
The administrator should explore the various hardware

options which are available from the network or the bibliographic utility and identify the equipment which will
satisfy the needs of the library.

Online terminals provide a wider range of features than do
dial-up terminals. Their capabilities will be specified by
the bibliographic utility, which may even be the supply
source for the terminals. If the library elects to use a
dial-up terminal, it has more flexibility in selecting the
model and manufacturer, and it can use the terminal for a
variety of other functions, such as online reference. The
dial-up terminal may not have all of the features contained
on the online terminal, such as the ability to display a
wide variety of characters, but it offers a good alternative for those institutions that have a lower volume of
cataloging and little need for specialized language
symbols.

7.3.3 Maintenance

There are maintenance charges associated with the hardware
purchased by the library, and such costs should be obtained
from the vendor. If the library elects to lease the
equipment, the library administrator should determine
whether the lease fee includes maintenance.

7.3.4 Computer Service Charges

There are no software maintenance costs associated with
online cataloging on a bibliographic cooperative; expenses
are bundled into the computer use costs. In the case of
OCLC, the FTU or first time use charge includes a number of
expenses, although there are additional charges for cards,
machine-readable tapes, and annual membership fees. These
costs can be obtained from the cooperative or the network.
Once unit charges are determined, the local library must
estimate the volume of cataloging to project total cost
during the year.

7.3.5 Communications Costs

Communications may be included in the computer service
charge or, in the case of dial-up, may represent an
additional item. Calculating these costs will require
information on current rates for the telecommunications
network and some sampling of typical cataloging times using
the online system. Either the utility or the network
should be able to provide some assistance in estimating
this expense.

7.3.6 Training and Documentation

Training is often provided as part of the services of the
bibliographic utility or the regional network, although
there could be an extra charge for this. That should be
determined by the administrator. To calculate staff costs,
the administrator must estimate the amount of training
necessary. The training site should be identified so any
travel expenses required may be calculated. Another
expense which could be included either under this category
or the next would be training and reference manuals. These
may be free or available at a charge. These will be
essential for reference use by the staff.

7.3.7 Supplies and Products

Supplies or products generated by an online cataloging
system may include catalog cards, machine-readable tapes,
directories, and statistical reports. The administrator
will need to identify those expenses based on unit costs
and volume. The exact expense will also be contingent on
how the library plans to use the cataloging information.
For example, if the library intends to apply the
bibliographic information to produce a COM catalog, it will
need cards only for those items which will not be included
in the COM catalog. The machine-readable tapes will
contain the data needed. If the library does not intend to
use it immediately, the tape will need to be inspected to
ensure there are no defects. The utilities may provide a

Not all libraries may elect to purchase machine-readable tapes of their cataloging, but such tapes are useful if the library intends to build a machine-readable database of its bibliographic holdings as a foundation for future automation projects. A number of the networks offer services to their members involving inspection or maintenance of these tapes.

In some instances, networks maintain subscriptions to machine-readable tapes containing the records of all their members and can select records for a specific institution if that library undertakes an automation project. This may not be a satisfactory arrangement for capturing current cataloging activity, since, for economy's sake, networks may elect to purchase tapes compiled on a semi-annual or quarterly basis.

7.3.8 Conversion

The major conversion expense for the library relates to the procedures the library employed prior to changing to online cataloging. There may be different standards between the library's cataloging and that found online, and it is generally up to the library to determine whether it wishes to accept these differences or modify the record to satisfy its policies and practices. Should the library elect to alter its records to conform, there could be a substantial conversion expense, which the library administrator will have to calculate, based on the degree of modification, labor to make the change, and the number of records.

Procedural changes may cause some unanticipated expense for the library, particularly if the staff involved in long-established procedures were not involved in the planning and decision-making process. Imposing a new procedure under these circumstances may result in resistance and/or employee turnover and the necessity to recruit and train new personnel. As with any change involving automation, it is wise to involve those who will have to implement the new procedure.

7.3.9 Retrospective Conversion

The library also will be faced with the option to
retrospectively convert all its bibliographic records,
since only those items cataloged on the bibliographic
utility system from the first day the library joins will
become part of the machine-readable file and be available
for use in a local automation project. Many libraries see
the value of retrospectively converting all of their
records to machine-readable form; several alternatives
exist in the event the library elects to do this. A
library can use the system to accomplish this itself,
entering bibliographic records and the library's holdings
symbol during those times when the terminal is not being
used for current cataloging, or it can contract for this
conversion.

Sample times can be taken to determine how long present
staff would require to enter present records, and the
number of records can also be estimated. This information
will provide the administrator with a basis for comparison
in considering the second alternative--contracting for
retrospective conversion. The networks or major utilities
may offer this as a special service and have special rates
for retrospective conversion. These can be obtained by the
library administrator as a basis for calculating this
expense. The network or utility can provide an estimate
for the total project based on the volume of records to be
converted and the time frame desired for converting them.

7.4 Computer Output Microform

Research has shown that COM is among the most common
products of automation in public libraries. [5] For larger
libraries a COM catalog can eliminate the need to maintain
large numbers of card catalogs in departments and branch
locations. Most cost studies in larger public libraries
have revealed substantial savings with COM, as well as good
public acceptance. In small- and medium-sized public
libraries, the major advantage of COM has been improved
access to local or regional holdings whenever the

application has been used on a cooperative basis. The
following costs are most frequently associated with COM:

1. Development of specifications
2. Hardware
3. Conversion
4. Equipment or furniture
5. Facilities remodeling
6. Ongoing computer services/production costs
7. Supplies and replacement

7.4.1 Developing Specifications

As with all automated applications, the library will have
to invest time in preparing specifications that define its
needs. COM offers the library options on "see" and "see
also" references (otherwise known as authority control) and
a variety of formats, typefaces, spacing between entries,
etc. The administrator or staff committee given
responsibility for developing specifications should review
the various options offered by the vendors, examine COM
catalogs developed by other libraries, and then build its
specifications based on that study.

There are also some key decisions regarding the microform
the library will use and the nature and frequency of
updates. COM catalogs are produced in microfiche or film
format. There are strong arguments for and supporters of
each format. Although fiche readers are less expensive,
many libraries claim that the motorized reel microfilm
readers are more convenient for the public.

The library will also have to decide on the frequency and
form of updates. A semiannual or quarterly update appears
to be common in many libraries, but this is not always a
recumulation of both old and new titles. The library may
wish to try several alternatives to determine the best
frequency. Some libraries have quarterly, semiannual, or
annual recumulations and alternate these with weekly or
monthly cumulations of new purchases. In any event, the
costs and the needs of the library in serving the public
will determine the best format and frequency.

7.4.2 Hardware

With COM there is no need to purchase computers or
terminals, since COM production is generally handled by
major vendors who can do this more economically than can an
individual library. The major expense will be the readers.
As previously noted, the choice is between microfiche and
film, with the latter being the more expensive. The volume
of use and the nature of the user will strongly influence
the decision. Microfiche readers may be selected if the
use is primarily by the staff, such as in a union catalog
employed for interlibrary loan service. Service may also
be a factor in the decision, since there are relatively few
manufacturers of motorized, high-speed film readers and a
substantially larger number of manufacturers of fiche
readers. The fact that there are fewer moving parts in
fiche readers provides greater reliability.

Other factors to consider in selecting COM readers, besides
cost, convenience, service, and reliability, are the number
of service units where the catalogs will be placed, the
size of the catalog, and the amount of use the readers will
experience. If the readers are intended to replace the
present card catalogs, then the number and location of the
readers will be defined, at least initially, by the
location of the card catalogs. Determining the number of
locations for a union COM catalog is another matter.
Location may be based upon the volume of interlibrary loan
traffic or reference service or other measures of the use
the library experiences. The size of the catalog will also
determine the number of readers the library may require,
particularly with film readers. Microfiche readers do not
have a limit on the maximum number of entries, but film
readers may. The reader manufacturers can provide
information on their current capacity. In the event the
catalog will not fit on one reader, then the library must
decide whether it will split the catalog in half or divide
it by subject and author-title or some other combination.
Finally, various formulas have been devised to aid in
estimating the number of readers needed to satisfy
particular traffic levels. These formulas are in the
literature, and information can be obtained from other
libraries that have adopted COM catalogs. Many COM vendors
will gladly supply lists of their customers who can serve
as sources for this information.

7.4.3 Conversion

Conversion expenses can be major for many libraries that
have no portion of their bibliographic records in
machine-readable form. There are several alternatives
available to libraries to avoid the necessity of converting
the library's shelflist. Some COM vendors have license to
use the files of major libraries or of the MARC service of
the Library of Congress. There is a strong likelihood of
duplication in public library collections, and it may be
possible to use various combinations of existing computer
files or microfilm records to build a machine-readable
database for a library by drawing upon the records of other
institutions. The library administrator should ask the
major COM suppliers for details and costs for any
conversion services they offer, and use this as a
foundation for calculations.

Other methods of conversion include use of a commercial
service bureau or the retrospective conversion services of
the major bibliographic utilities, as well as the lease of
equipment to allow the library's staff to undertake this
conversion themselves. Use of a commercial service bureau
will necessitate design of a computer program to manage the
converted data; that is equally true if the library leases
its own equipment. There are, therefore, considerable
advantages in drawing upon the conversion services of the
COM vendor or using the retrospective conversion services
of the utilities.

Orientation for the public and staff is a form of
conversion expense as well. While most readers, fiche or
film, are designed for ease of use and often have
instructions, some patrons will require assistance. The
catalog format will probably require some interpretation,
since the use of location codes is common. Just as the
card catalog required some staff and public orientation,
the COM catalog must be effectively publicized and
instructional materials, and perhaps some signs, may be
needed to reduce confusion and ensure effective
utilization. Again, the experience of other libraries may
be a useful planning guide.

7.4.4 Furniture

Furniture is an expense that is often forgotten in
calculating costs for COM. The planned locations should be
inspected to determine whether the readers can be placed on
existing equipment. Consideration should be given to
special heights required for children and those in
wheelchairs. If the library intends to replace the card
catalog, then the COM readers can logically be placed in
the former location of these units. That will require the
purchase of tables for this purpose, unless counters are
preferred. Some libraries may wish to acquire chairs for
the convenience for those who will be consulting the
catalog at some length. In addition, some libraries may
elect to purchase reader-printers to allow patrons to
search and duplicate sections of the catalog as a basis for
compiling bibliographies or for ease in searching.
Additional furniture may be required to house this
equipment.

7.4.5 Remodeling

Some remodeling of the facilities may be required even for
COM. Since readers require electrical power, the
administrator will have to survey the area where the
readers will be placed to determine whether additional
outlets are needed. While COM readers seldom have special
power requirements or demand special lines, the number of
readers may require a change in electrical service entrance
equipment, particularly in older libraries with limited
circuits.

Another consideration is lighting. While most microform
readers are designed to function in a variety of lighting
conditions, the best source of light comes from the side.
Many users prefer a lower light level to optimize their use
of the readers. The administrator should preview the model
reader to be selected in a number of settings
representative of light levels common to actual locations
to determine whether some adjustments may be necessary.
Sometimes the solution may be to remove bulbs from
multi-bulb fixtures. In other instances, a more elaborate
solution may be required. Library maintenance staff or
electrical contractors should be able to estimate costs and

materials necessary for this remodeling. Glare from nearby windows may also be a problem. If so, the problem can be alleviated or eliminated by proper placement of the equipment and by the use of window coverings.

7.4.6 Ongoing Service Costs

After conversion to the COM catalog, the library has to budget for ongoing COM production costs. Generally, the vendor will segregate costs into conversion, computer time for manipulation of the files, additions to the database, the COM process itself, and the cost for microfiche or film. Each vendor is likely to package its services in a variety of ways. The major point is that the library will need to gain an estimate of those charges based on the frequency of update and generation of COM products.

7.4.7 Supplies and Replacement

Supplies for COM include light bulbs and service and cleaning materials. Certain public relations materials, such as descriptive brochures produced to help orient the public, could also be included. Finally, there will be expenses in making periodic replacement or repair of the readers. Some manufacturers may have maintenance plans to defer eventual replacement cost, but it would be wise for the administrator to budget some funds for ongoing replacement of the readers, particularly in high volume areas.

7.5 Online Circulation Control

Since online circulation control is one of the more complex applications, the library administrator would be advised to spend time consulting some of the specialized guides devoted solely to the planning of and conversion to online circulation control. Some major cost elements can be isolated in estimating preliminary costs:

1.   Preparation of specifications
2.   Hardware and software
3.   Maintenance
4.   Communications
5.   Supplies
6.   Operating personnel
7.   Conversion and training
8.   Remodeling

7.5.1 Developing Specifications

Any library planning to employ online circulation control
would be advised to invest time and expense in gathering
information from other libraries and vendors as well as
consulting the literature as a basis for preparing its
specifications. Larger installations frequently make use
of consultants to prepare specifications for their
institution and to assist the library in the evaluation of
bids and proposals.

7.5.2 Hardware and Software

Such an application is likely to employ at least a
minicomputer and require a specially written software
program. These expenses can be obtained from the vendors.
If the system is a turnkey application, and the library is
seeking some modifications in the standard package to
satisfy its special needs, then some allowance for this
should be made when the quotes are reviewed. There are
some microcomputer-based circulation systems and also some
systems which employ a minicomputer which interacts with a
larger central computer to perform functions which cannot
be handled locally. The administrator will need to
determine whether the system being purchased will require
some additional ongoing supportive computer services and
include that cost in the calculations.

7.5.3 Maintenance

Maintenance costs for both hardware and software are
expenses in online circulation control systems. To reduce
the frequency or extent of downtime, an option which some

libraries may consider is the purchase of spare equipment,
such as terminals, barcode or optical character reading
devices, and similar items with a high likelihood of
breakdown.

Backup systems represent another expense. While libraries
often design manual backup procedures, some turnkey system
manufacturers offer equipment which can operate
independently for charging and discharging materials and
will permit transfer of this captured data once the
computer is running again.

There is no hard and fast formula for these expenses. Some
information can be gained through discussions and
observations in other libraries. While maintenance costs
for hardware and software should be clearly established by
the vendor or the manufacturer, the need for spare parts or
backup equipment really depends upon the reliability,
degree of use, and amount and degree of care used in
operating the system.

7.5.4 Communications

Communications expense will depend upon the number of
locations using the hardware. A multibranch system or
cooperative will experience telephone line charges and
require lease or purchase of equipment associated with
communications. In some instances, even a single location
circulation control system may require the lease of
telephone lines. Some manufacturers maintain their
hardware and software through telephone access to the
system. While this is customarily done on a dial-up basis,
some manufacturers may require leased lines. The
administrator should obtain information from the vendor
regarding any communications expenses. In proposals or
specifications, the vendor should be required to define
these costs and supply a recommended network for the
terminals. Frequently, the local telephone company can
also provide consultant service in recommending data
networks appropriate for the application.

7.5.5 Supplies

Supplies are likely to be a significant expense in online
circulation control because of the changes which may be
required in forms and the increased frequency of production
of certain types of notices and reports. In some
instances, it may be possible to employ existing forms,
such as borrowers' cards, but any notices which are
generated by the computer are likely to be new.
Calculating this expense involves estimating the volume of
supplies which will be consumed and the unit costs. Some
vendors of packaged turnkey systems also offer supplies as
a sideline. In other instances, it may be necessary for
the library to design its own forms and make arrangements
with a local printer qualified to produce computer forms.
Another alternative would be to join forces with other
libraries that have purchased the system and adopt forms
that can be used by a number of different libraries.

7.5.6 Operating Personnel

Unlike online cataloging and COM, online circulation
control will necessitate expenses for operating personnel.
While many vendors advertise the fact that their systems
require little or no operating support, this is
unrealistic. There are certain procedures involved in
starting the system each day, preserving records,
generating notices and forms, and shutting the system down.
While this may involve only a part-time assignment in a
small or medium-sized library, it still represents an
expense. If the administrator cannot learn the personnel
requirements for supporting a turnkey system, or feels
uncomfortable with the information received, conferring
with other libraries that have similar equipment may be the
most reliable way of determining or confirming personnel
needs. Some insight will also be needed as to the level of
skill required to support the system. If the library can
use existing staff for this work, after training in the
procedures, the administrator will need to determine
whether the vendor will provide this training and whether
there will be an additional expense for it. It would also
be well to identify whether this training is readily
available, and at what expense, in the event of employee
turnover.

7.5.7 Conversion and Training

Conversion represents one of the more significant expenses
in online circulation control. If the library already has
its bibliographic records in machine-readable form, most
turnkey systems are now designed to permit this tape record
of the database to be loaded into the computer memory.
Nonetheless, the administrator should request the vendor to
supply details and costs for conversion services. Besides
the conversion of the library's bibliographic records and
holdings information, the major steps include the
development of the patron file and the inventorying and
labeling of the collection. Both of those routines can be
estimated based on sampling using the steps recommended by
the manufacturer or information obtained from other
libraries or from the literature. There are a host of
alternative methods for converting the library to online
circulation control. The major guideline is to select the
procedure which offers the least number of manual steps as
that will generally be the most economical and the least
prone to error. Cleaning up errors can add significantly
to conversion costs.

Training for personnel is an expense which must be
calculated as both one-time and ongoing. The vendor may
include a specified amount of training in the cost of the
system, but it is rare to find a vendor who will train new
personnel hired because of normal turnover. If the library
must assume that responsibility, some expense will be
associated with the production of materials and training
personnel. Staff time involved in training is also an
expense and, while it is necessary and justifiable, it can
become significant.

7.5.8 Remodeling

Online circulation systems do not usually require
significant remodeling expense, but that depends on the
environmental requirements of the minicomputer and the
power supply and cabling for the terminals. An older
building with few or no ducts for cables may necessitate
substantial work. Discussions with the vendor to determine
power and environmental requirements and an architectural
or engineering inspection of the library should allow some

estimates of this expense. Often some public service desks
may lack sufficient power for terminals, or the circulation
desk may need remodeling; that can be assessed through
personal inspection by the library administrator.

7.6 Acquisitions

Calculating the expenses associated with automated
acquisitions is difficult because of the variety of ways
this can be accomplished. Some of the major bibliographic
cooperatives, such as OCLC, offer it as a separate
subsystem. Some of the major book jobbers offer online or
package off-site systems. Some of the turnkey circulation
control systems offer acquisitions modules. Some standard
cost factors can be considered for any type of acquisitions
system:

1. Development of specifications
2. Hardware and software
3. Maintenance
4. Communications
5. Supplies
6. Conversion and training

Usually the most complex aspect of acquisitions is the
integration of the system with the library's selection,
cataloging, and accounting procedures. For that reason,
development of acquisitions specifications is very much a
detailed and custom-design activity. Whether the library
will require purchase or lease of hardware and software
depends on the alternative selected by the institution. If
the library elects to integrate acquisitions with online
cataloging, there may be no additional expense involved,
particularly if existing computer terminals and printers
can be employed. If not, then the purchase price of those
items and their maintenance must be calculated.

If the acquisitions system is integrated with the library's
book purchasing procedures through a jobber, there will
probably be a hardware expense for a terminal, and possibly
a printer, along with maintenance. Some firms offer
package acquisitions software which can be operated on
local hardware owned by the library or local government.
That is usually economical only for larger libraries, and

there are expenses associated with obtaining the software,
maintaining it, and running it on either the library's
computer or a third party's computer. Mounting an
acquisitions module onto a turnkey circulation system will
necessitate the purchase of a software package and usually
a hardware upgrade for the minicomputer. (This latter
aspect depends on the capacity of the system.) The
administrator should obtain an estimate from the vendor for
these hardware and software costs as well as for the
maintenance expenses.

Communications costs may be associated with some types of
automated acquisitions systems. For example, the online
systems offered by the jobbers may be dial-up or online,
depending on traffic; either alternative represents an
expense which can be estimated. The subsystems offered by
the bibliographic utilities may avoid this expense if
cataloging is already performed online. If the library
employs dial-up, then there will be a charge.

Supplies associated with automated acquisitions are
generally a nominal expense, but it is likely that order
forms will change. Some systems avoid forms and transmit
order information to the jobbers or suppliers in
machine-readable form for processing by the vendor's
computer. The administrator will need to identify the form
of product generated by the system and determine how that
can be adapted to the library's present selection,
cataloging, and accounting procedures. The acquisitions
service vendor may furnish standard forms for the library,
or the library may design special forms.

Conversion and training are unlikely to represent
significant expenses, but there will be procedures which
will be altered and some time will be needed for staff to
gain familiarity with the application. Both the expense
and the time required depend on how complicated the process
of integrating the system with the library's present
methods is. In any event, the administrator should
determine whether the vendor will provide training and
identify steps which can be taken in the event of employee
turnover in this function.

7.7 Business Services

Estimating the cost of automating business services, such
as word processing, accounting, and payroll, is also
difficult because of the alternatives which a library can
employ. Many of these services are so common that they can
be provided economically through local computer service
bureaus, or contracted for through larger libraries. Many
mini- and even microcomputer-based systems are available
for outright purchase; several of the turnkey library
systems offer modules that allow the addition of these
common services. Calculating the costs of automated
business services usually involves the following factors:

1. Preparation of specifications
2. Hardware and software
3. Maintenance
4. Telecommunications
5. Supplies
6. Conversion and training

Because of the availability of so many packages and
options, some time will be required to identify those
automated business services which best suit the library's
needs and integrate well with established procedures. If
the library does not have any computerized equipment and
wishes to avoid maintenance and capital expenditures, then
it may be best to purchase its services from a service
bureau or another library. In some instances, it may be
possible to achieve this through dial-up. In this
alternative, however, the library must assume some
communications expenses, although these may be relatively
minor if the line is local. Purchase of a computer
terminal and a modem will be required, coupled with a
maintenance agreement, but this may be significantly less
expensive than a mini- or microcomputer package system.

A number of specialized applications, however, may lend
themselves to the latter alternative. For example, some
library cooperatives or larger libraries have acquired
microcomputer graphics design systems for production of
public relations items. There may be little or no need for
this system to interface with other applications used by
the library. Word processing systems are also frequently
sold separately. Their cost has become so low through the

demand generated by business and industry that it may be more economical for the library to consider their purchase as a separate package rather than attempt to integrate this application with other systems owned by the library.

In business services, the more common the application, the greater the variety of options. The task of the administrator is to weigh the relative costs for hardware, software, maintenance, communications costs, and miscellaneous expenses to reach a decision. Supplies are sometimes a factor, but most business systems have considerable flexibility. The administrator should determine whether the system will require or consume comparatively costly materials to perform its function. Conversion expenses in the use of business systems are usually procedural in nature, but training can become a factor if the mini- or microcomputer systems come with only one or two software applications. This is often the case with such packages, and it is desirable to make additional use of the system. A manufacturer may develop a specific piece of hardware and design an application for it, such as word processing. The library may know the hardware has the capacity and flexibility for other business procedures but staff lack the programming skills to develop those applications, and the manufacturer either has no intentions to prepare additional software or is not planning to initiate this software design until some future date.

7.8 Summary

Estimating automation costs requires collecting data on the time and expense involved with decision making and preparing specifications or proposals, hardware and software purchase costs, maintenance expenses, communications, remodeling of facilities, furniture and/or miscellaneous equipment, supplies, operating personnel, insurance, archival storage, conversion and training, and replacement.

Preliminary estimates on these costs can be obtained from vendors, manufacturers, software design firms, commercial service bureaus, other libraries, and the literature. Estimates can be confirmed through the issuance of RFPs (requests for proposals) and the development of formal

specifications and bidding documents. In the event the
bids exceed the original quotation by a substantial amount,
it is possible for the library to reject any or all bids
through the inclusion of appropriate language in its
instructions to bidders and advertisements.

RFPs generally describe a need or problem and require the
vendor to provide a detailed solution and quote a price for
the hardware, software, and associated expenses. To
construct a sound RFP, the library must clearly describe
the need or problem, provide information on the volume of
the activity, define any required standards the vendor will
have to meet, and contain sufficient information to guide
the vendor in submitting a price. Formal purchase
contracts are another means of obtaining exact costs.
These are much more detailed and prescribe specific
procedures or equipment to be supplied by the vendor. They
may contain specifications of a functional nature;
alternatively, they may specify that equipment proposed be
equal or comparable to a specific manufacturer and model
cited. The formal purchase contract will include
instructions to bidders, a contract which will define any
penalties or deadlines, the formal specifications, and bid
and bond forms to permit accurate evaluation of the price
and terms and bind the vendor to completion of the project.

Several examples of automated applications have been
discussed, namely online cataloging, COM, circulation
control, acquisitions, and business services, to illustrate
what expenses should be considered and how they may be
determined as a basis for decision making.

8

Assessing Factors Other Than Cost

It is the responsibility of library administration to
measure costs and determine the most economical method of
operation wherever possible. After reading the preceding
chapters, the administrator may conclude that there are so
many costs associated with automation that the present
manual procedures employed might better be continued.
Other factors besides cost, however, must be considered in
decision making. After all, the purpose of the public
library is not just to save tax funds through its operating
procedures; there are some responsibilities that outweigh
cost. This chapter will identify some of these concerns
and provide a means for objectively weighing them alongside
cost.

At the beginning of this guide, A Planning Process for
Public Libraries was recommended as a means to direct the
logical collection of information pertinent to providing
better library service and the development of procedures
which facilitate writing and implementing long-range plans,
goals, objectives, and strategies. Such a plan should
grant the library a solid foundation for using automation,
for there are a number of qualities associated with the use
of this technology which should contribute significantly to
achieving the goals defined by the library.

Before considering those qualities, however, it may be well
to point out that some of the costs associated with
automation are the direct result of the deficiencies of
present manual methods. For example, inventorying the
collection is a desirable step in assessing the extent of

loss. If manual procedures were effective in controlling
the collection, this step might not be needed. Online
circulation control systems permit the holdings of the
library to be more easily maintained. Another example is
the need to correct deficiencies in the library's
bibliographic records as a preparatory step to converting
this data to machine-readable form. While it is possible
that these same errors may recur once these functions are
automated, it is more likely that the automated procedures
will eliminate many of the opportunities for error and
allow easier correction.

8.1 Considering Factors Other Than Cost

This leads naturally to the first noncost factor
characteristic of automation--improved quality of service.
For example, online cataloging allows the library to
benefit from what is generally conceded to be better
quality bibliographic control. Online circulation control
enables the library to more rapidly notify patrons when
materials they have reserved are available, or to remind
them when resources should be returned or renewed. The
serials control system will provide greater insight to the
nature of the library's holdings and assist the library in
filling gaps in its collection. Online reference services
allow the library to offer much more information to its
clientele than previous manual methods. While it is hard
to place a dollar value on quality, there is little
question that it has value. The public should have genuine
concern that public services represent solid value in
return for their tax investment.

In fulfilling its responsibilities to its community, the
library regularly buys many resources which are
comparatively costly. An expensive art book collection may
be developed, for example, simply because it would be
extremely costly for a single family or patron to acquire
these materials. The library could save considerable funds
by not purchasing any art books, but it has an obligation
to ensure that its community has access to resources of all
types within the constraints of its budget. It would also
be more economical for the library to avoid the expense
involved with children's story hours. Nonetheless,
libraries offer this as a means to introduce more children

to the pleasures of reading and to attract them and their
parents to the library.

It can be argued that the library, or any cultural
institution, exists to save tax dollars, since it can
purchase and preserve materials and make them accessible to
the entire community at little or no direct expense. It is
doubtful, however, that any library director ever used this
logic to justify the purchase of a special collection on
the Elizabethan theater or that an art museum curator
applied the same logic to the acquisition of a rare
Rembrandt.

While determining the role of a public library properly
rests with its governance and board, based on sound
community analysis and the professional recommendations of
its staff, it is generally conceded that, among other
responsibilities, the institution performs the function of
informing, educating, and culturally enriching the people
it serves. General statistics reveal that only 25-30
percent of the population of any area is registered and
regularly uses the public library. To ensure that the full
community is aware of its resources and is attracted to use
them, a public library generally has strong outreach
efforts and public information programs. It frequently
offers programs and services designed to attract a group,
such as the elderly, that may not regularly use the
library.

It would be more economical to eliminate those efforts; it
may even be possible to demonstrate that only small numbers
of nonusers are attracted by them. On the other hand, if
the library failed to take this initiative and concerned
itself only with satisfying the demands of the minority who
regularly use its services, that institution would not be
fulfilling its obligation to serve the entire community.
The purpose of the public library is not to save money, but
to spend its revenues wisely to satisfy the needs of the
entire community. The library's long-range development
plan should reflect these ends. If the plan is soundly
prepared, based on community analysis and input from a
variety of representative groups, that should be
justification enough.

Another factor characteristic of automation is improved
accessibility. There is little question that online
circulation or cataloging present the opportunity for
greater access, not only to the local library's holdings,
but also to the holdings of other participating libraries
if the automated system is a cooperative effort. Improved
accessibility means better use of local resources and the
avoidance of expenditures for infrequently used resources
which can be obtained from other libraries and that can be
translated into tangible benefits for the community. It
may be difficult to place a dollar value on this
characteristic, but no one will doubt the advantage it
provides the local library. While larger libraries may not
feel the need to draw upon the resources of others through
online cataloging or circulation control, those
applications give institutions greater control of their own
materials. In actuality, however, few libraries are able
to rely solely on their own resources to satisfy all the
requirements of their communities. Information is growing
too rapidly, and the expense of acquiring and organizing it
demands a cooperative approach to conserve tax dollars.
Automation lends itself to cooperative resource sharing
much more efficiently than manual procedures.

A third quality of automation is currency. Many manual
methods occasioned long delays between the acquisition of
information or resources and their availability to the
public. With many applications of automation, that delay
is substantially or significantly reduced. Through
effective integration of automated processes, it is
possible to order a title on an acquisitions system, enter
the bibliographic data in the cataloging system, and note
in the circulation system that the item is on order and
permit patrons to place reserves on it. Online reference
service allows the user to have access to abstracts and
bibliographic and nonbibliographic information long before
the data will be available in print, depending upon the
update frequency of the various databases.

Related to currency is the amount of time that it takes for
certain automated tasks to be completed relative to manual
procedures. Prior to the introduction of cooperative
online cataloging, it was common for public libraries to
have large backlogs requiring many months to process.
Today, a typical public library locates nearly 94 percent

of its purchases already cataloged on the system, thereby substantially reducing its cataloging backlog and assuring timely delivery to the public. While certain aspects of online circulation control, such as charge in and charge out, require about the same time as the traditional manual methods, the system automatically provides much more rapid notification to patrons of their reserves and overdues; this timeliness is respected and appreciated by the public. The amount of time that is saved through automation may be difficult to convert into tax savings because of the many fixed expenses the institution may have. Nonetheless, the computer has the ability to accomplish certain tasks in nanoseconds compared with the minutes or hours required for performance of similar tasks through manual means.

Many libraries experiencing growth in various aspects of their service, such as circulation, also benefit through the introduction of automation to avoid hiring additional personnel. For example, while an online circulation control system may not necessarily reduce personnel in a small or medium-sized library because of the variety of tasks performed by those individuals, the system will allow the same number of persons to cope with increased circulation in the future. The same holds true for automated acquisitions, serials, and cataloging systems. It may not be possible to eliminate personnel through the introduction of these systems, but if the collection is projected to grow at a more rapid rate than the present, automation will help existing personnel cope with those increases or enable them to direct their attention to other tasks.

Accuracy is another quality of automation, since it can be used to reduce the number of human interventions in any process. While it is true that entering incorrect information will render any system, manual or automated, useless or ineffective, it is possible for automated systems to guard against this. For example, light-activated wands, scanners, or barcode readers may be employed in automated circulation to eliminate incorrect entry of borrower information. Programs can be written to guard against inversion of numbers in data entry. Multiple files can provide assurance that incorrect bibliographic entry will be weeded out of certain cataloging functions. Mainly, however, automation serves to reduce the amount of human interaction in repetitive tasks that are particularly prone to error.

Automation also affords many opportunities to make better use of existing human resources, allow job enrichment to occur, and grant the individual employee greater control over his or her work environment. That should lead to a staff better qualified to serve the public or perform their assigned function and aid in the reduction of employee turnover. There may be some staff who will feel threatened by the introduction of automation, and there may be those who will resist its application, but it is possible for management to resolve those problems through participatory techniques and effective training. Generally, staff members who see that the institution is willing to make an investment in them and involve them in decisions affecting their work and the design of the institution's goals will not only accept automation, but will feel enriched because of it.

Increasingly, the key to maintaining or improving budgets in the public sector is better management information; this can be provided with automation. The effective manager must have solid information to document the needs of his or her agency, and the computer has remarkable qualities for compiling data. One of the more frustrating factors in many manual circulation systems is the very limited insight those methods permit into the use of the collection and the nature of the library's users. A typical online circulation system, on the other hand, enables management to identify less frequently used resources as a basis for weeding, highlights titles in high demand to permit rapid ordering of needed duplicates, and permits the redesign of the library's collection development program to ensure higher turnover, among many other things. These data can be used to justify new services and increased appropriations for high demand resources. The increased productivity of personnel should also warrant salary adjustments.

These are only a few of the factors associated with automation which should be considered along with cost in reaching a decision on automation. Since it is only in some instances that a dollar value can be placed on some of these factors, the question that arises in most library

administrators' minds is how they can be evaluated
objectively. This question is addressed in the final
section of this chapter.

8.2 Evaluating Factors Other Than Cost

There are a variety of methods which management science has
developed or adopted to measure relative worth, but all the
theories require a reference point--something to which
specific factors can be compared. The best reference point
for a library is its long-range plan of development, for it
reveals the goals and priorities of the institution and
strategies for satisfying those goals. This is why such a
plan is necessary and why libraries are encouraged to
employ the procedures in <u>A Planning Process for Public
Libraries</u>. The library's general long-range plan should
indicate those factors which most influence the direction
the institution should take in improving its services to
the community, hence its usefulness as a basis for
establishing priorities in the plan for automation.

The library administrator or planning committee should
examine those automation projects being proposed for the
institution and look at the qualities that were defined for
establishing priorities. By this time, it may be possible
to add more factors, such as those described in this
chapter. The committee should arrive at a list of 5 to 12
qualities or factors which automation will provide. A
table should again be prepared listing the qualities or
factors in separate columns across the top and the
abbreviated long-range goals in separate lines on the left
of the table. Table 2, which follows this section, is an
example.

Assume at this point that all the qualities, such as
currency, access, etc., are of relatively equal weight.
For scoring purposes, establish a scale of values 1 to 5 or
1 to 10 or some other appropriate range--with 1 as the low
value. Now take each goal and evaluate the contribution
that the individual qualities or factors will make toward
achieving that goal, and place that relative score in the
appropriate column. Do this for each of the goals. When
all of the factors have been assigned weights, add the
totals in the columns for each of the qualities or factors.

If a planning committee is involved, it may be valuable to
perform this exercise individually or jointly, depending
upon the preference of the group, and arrive at either a
group total or an average. The result will be weighted
factors which will aid in comparing costs.

It may be determined that online circulation control is
more costly than the manual procedure currently employed,
but the online system affords greater accessibility, better
quality public service, more rapid service, and accuracy.
Furthermore, in the context of the library's long-range
plan, these factors rank as the more important elements in
contributing to the furtherance of those goals.

Conversely, it may be determined that online reference is
substantially more costly than traditional procedures.
However, it affords currency and has greater impact upon
the public. In the context of the library's long-range
plan, these factors may rank as the least important
elements contributing to the furtherance of the library's
goals. The cost may therefore outweigh the positive
features of the service.

While this method will require some refinement for each
library, it provides a framework for considering factors
which cannot readily be assigned a dollar value, and it
should be of help in the justification of projects and in
decision making.

TABLE 2.   Evaluating Factors Other Than Cost

	QUALITIES/FACTORS ASSOCIATED WITH SERVICE				
	Quality of Service	Accessibility	Currency	Timeliness	Growth of Resources
ABBREVIATED LIBRARY GOALS					
Expansion of Service to Disadvantaged	4	3	1	1	1
Enlarging Reference Collection	5	2	4	1	5
Satisfaction of Patron Reserves	5	5	3	5	4
Developing Staff Abilities	5	2	2	1	5
Opening Three Branches in New Areas of County	1	3	1	1	5
Total Weight	20	15	11	9	20

9

Afterword

It is the intention of this guide to furnish public library administrators, particularly those in medium and small communities, with some procedures and guidelines which will help them to more effectively reach decisions on automation—how to evaluate it, how to plan for it, and how to more accurately estimate some of the costs associated with it. The last chapter considers factors other than cost.

There are many demands upon the tax dollar these days. There are even more pressures upon the public library's revenues. Often an administrator defers needed change because the economy or local trends dictate remaining with the status quo. Services and procedures continue as they are until better times and circumstances prevail. Unfortunately, it is when times are most difficult that the administrator must be the most innovative. If there are limitations upon the library's revenues, that dictates a need for change so existing resources can be better employed.

While automation may, in some instances, require a substantial investment and greater expense than present procedures, it is essential that the administrator recall that his or her responsibility is to ensure that the institution expends its resources wisely to satisfy the needs of its public. That may require an investment in the future of the library and the community; with the tangible advantages automation promises, there are few wiser expenditures.

References

1. U.S. National Center for Educational Statistics. Library general information survey (LIBGIS III) public libraries, 1977-78 (Advance report in photocopy) Washington, D.C.: National Center for Education Statistics; 1982.

2. Palmour, Vernon E.; Bellassai, Marcia C.; De Wath, Nancy V. A planning process for public libraries. Chicago: American Library Association; 1980.

3. Dowlin, Kenneth E. Maggie's Place, Pikes Peak active computer environment. Colorado Springs, CO: Pikes Peak Regional Library District; 1979.

4. Lynch, Mary Jo. Financing online search services in publicly supported libraries: The report on an ALA survey. Chicago: American Library Association; 1981.

5. Sager, Donald J. The American public library. Dublin, OH: OCLC Online Computer Library Center, Inc.; 1982.

Suggested Reading

Are you a convert? Conversion strategies and costs. Illinois Libraries. 62(7); 609-633; 1980 September.

Atherton, Pauline; Christian, Roger W. Librarians and online services. New York: Knowledge Industry Publications, Inc.; 1977.

Bahr, Alice H. Automated library circulation systems, 1979-1980. 2d ed. White Plains, NY: Knowledge Industry Publications, Inc.; 1979.

Boss, Richard W. The library manager's guide to automation. White Plains, NY: Knowledge Industry Publications, Inc.; 1979.

Butler, Brett; Aveney, Brian; Scholz, William. The conversion of manual catalogs to collection databases. Library Technology Reports. 14(2): 109-206; 1978 March/April.

Computer law: purchasing, leasing, and licensing hardware, software, and services. New York: Practising Law Institute; 1980.

Corbin, John. Developing computer-based library systems. Phoenix, AZ: Oryx Press; 1981.

Covvey, H. Dominic; McAlister, Neil Harding. Computer consciousness: Surviving the automated 80s. Reading, MA: Addison-Wesley Publishing Co.; 1980. Crismond, Linda F.

Quality issues in retrospective conversion projects.
Library Resources & Technical Services. 25(1): 48-55; 1981
January/March.

Financing online search services in publicly supported
libraries: the report of an ALA survey. Chicago: American
Library Assoc.; 1981.

Fosdick, Howard. Computer basics for libraries and
information scientists. Arlington, VA: Information
Resources Press; 1981.

Grosch, Audrey N. Minicomputers in libraries, 1979-80.
White Plains, NY: Knowledge Industry Publications, Inc.;
1979.

Hayes, Robert; Becker, Joseph. Handbook of data processing
for libraries. 2d ed. Los Angeles: Melville Publishing Co.;
1974.

Hoover, Ryan E. The library and information manager's guide
to online services. White Plains, NY: Knowledge Industry
Publications, Inc.; 1980.

Katz, Bill; Clifford, Anne, eds. Reference and online
services handbook: Guidelines, policies, and procedures for
libraries. New York: Neal-Schuman Publishers, Inc.; 1982.

Kimber, R.T. Automation in libraries. 2d ed. New York:
Pergamon Press; 1974.

Martin, James. An end-user's guide to data base. Englewood
Cliffs, NJ: Prentice-Hall, Inc.; 1981.

Martin, S.K. Library networks, 1981-1982. White Plains, NY:
Knowledge Industry Publications, Inc.; 1981.

Matthews, Joseph R. Choosing an automated library system: A
planning guide. Chicago: American Library Assoc.; 1980.

Meadow, Charles T.; Cochrane, Pauline (Atherton). Basics of
online searching. New York: John Wiley and Sons; 1981.

Requests for proposals: preparation guidelines for data processing applications. Greenlawn, NY: Dyna Systems; 1981.

Rorvig, Mark E. Microcomputers and libraries: A guide to technology, products and applications. White Plains, NY: Knowledge Industry Publications, Inc.; 1981.

Index